COULD THE MILLENNIALS GENERATION BE THE GREATEST EVER?

By: Ramon Kleier

RoseDog Books
PITTSBURGH, PENNSYLVANIA 15238

RoseDog Books
585 Alpha Drive
Suite 103
Pittsburgh, PA 15222
Visit our website at www.rosedogbookstore.com

ISBN: 978-1-64913-045-7
eISBN: 978-1-64913-038-9

Dear Readers:
(What a coincident!)

A short time ago, I decided to write about my generation. I couldn't recall anyone writing a manuscript about "WHY" our generation was crowned; "The Greatest Generation!"

Unfortunately, when I tapped that very first word on my keyboard, I was unaware that: Soon, very soon, "Evil" would be lurking in the shadows!"

At that point (pre "Evil" lurking), I began by lambasting today's leaders of our country, in 20/20. Including the entire swamp, and it's beaches!

The world was spinning out of control. Chapter One was attributed to what a terrible state of morality and hopelessness, of our divided country over the past few years.

My dad always told us never argue about politics or religion.

However, circumstance of our present leaders of our country, must be address in order for me to compare my generation to today's, and all generations.

The entire legislators of our country…BOTH SIDES…were combative six months before this president was sworn in! That was just the beginning! It has been worsening since then.

"Tweets" were the talk of the day and night, and the wee hours of the morning. There was name calling, there was lying, dishonesty, immorality, sexual related affairs, traitors, unpatriotic slander, belittling, lying under oath! The moral fabric of our country has been ripped to pieces!

Hatred fills the air, spewing gusher style. "BOTH SIDES" cannot agree on even the 'interpretation' of the laws.

There were impeachment procedures against the sitting president! Criminality flourished. A few were indicted and went to prison. There were many more that should have been put in that same cell.

The ones whom never went to prison, were as guilty as the ones who are locked down? Only because of the 'specific's' of laws were not clearly 'politically correct'! Most disturbing of all, the entire swamp is ambient with hostility.

The top three legislator's leaders, of the largest, free country in the world, were not on 'speaking terms with each other!' Venom is oozing every time they part their lips. They are our leaders! World leaders! It's frightening, that 'both sides' do not have anyone with the 'stones' to stand up for sanity, righteousness, and respect for our own brothers and sisters.

The good ol' *BOYS* of politics are still alive and well? Or? Are they? "HUM?"

Today's legislature reminds me of a flock of spineless yellow belly sap suckers! They don't want to face the *REAL* world!

It's a "Barnum and Bailey" world, the tents are up filled to the gill, with puppets, just as phony as it can be, BUT! It wouldn't be make believe IF WE BELIEVED in them!

Bullying is rampant! Our ears are blasted with one lie after the other. And everybody seems to be: Stiffed necked!

Hindsight: Maybe we should blame ourselves? WE put them in their positions.

The Constitution of the United States/Amendments are well past; "Out Dated!" Expiration Code: The twentieth century.

For the first few years of this administration, they fought insanely, and insistently, on a daily basis, dividing our country. Impeachment was finally filed. The impeachment procedures put all legislative activity on the back burner.

They were blindsided by the fact that millions of Chinese were seen worldwide on social medium, wearing mask!

Evidently, that foreseeable disaster didn't seem to faze the swamp? No one suggested to take action of any kind. OR? Did they already know of it?

Records do show, that respected agencies did indeed alert the White House and The Pentagon! Of a possible deadly virus world wide, many months earlier!

Unfortunately, our leaders were too busy defaming each other! Suddenly, "EVIL" burst out of the shadows! The dreaded; COVID-19 hit the ground running at full speed.

At this time, the 'projections' of deaths could be up to a million Americans! With all of the present turmoil, 'estimates' of death for the future are like 'tumble weed' swirling and bouncing in the wind.

They want to blame the World Health Organization for the same reason. They will penalize the WHO by 'freezing' our contributions, and commitment of financial support…reportedly, many millions of dollars! Right in the midst of a deadly virus ever known to mankind!!!

That takes me back to The Garden, when Adam threw Eve under the bus.

Of course, tomorrow's version of what was said today, most likely, will change? At the time of these writings, a crash course of controlling a virus of this magnitude, is ongoing. Again, legislative activities has been swept under the rug.

Nobody knows how to combat this killer, it's dubbed as the 'invisible enemy.' It has sent our country into total chaos!

In a nutshell, this administration was 'damage goods' from the on set. Russia and Ukraine were suspected of interfering with our election and the impeachment process. And now add COVID-19 to the mix. Bad timing C-19!

Federal Government agencies are arguing with local governors, about who should have priority over securing proper medical equipment to fight this battle! During these difficult times, local and federal governments, are bidding against each other, in procuring the materials and equipment during a state of emergency!

Guess what? The Governors are being blamed for this debacle? What a price (for us, the people) to pay for political 'gains.'

Today, April 12, 20/20, is Easter Sunday! 99.9% of the Christian world cannot go to their place of worship, because of spreading COVID-19. We cannot gather together.

There is a 'war' now between those same legislators, and the congregations of churches, all over the country, and world.
Is this a 'three ring circus, or what?'

Those .01% of 'Christians' will conduct their services anyway!
First amendment rights! Another can of worms unleashed!

Based on past records, it shows that when numbers of people gather, there will be numbers of people who will be infected by the deadly virus. It's described as, a blast from a shotgun! I believe, it's more like playing Russian Roulette with eight rounds in the chamber! Many more people will die…who weren't even there, maybe their own family member's at home!

How can our own Constitution *'Hypothetically'…in these circumstances…the new norm…'protect' assassins?*

In addition, deaths will also come from the lack of food!

As of today, Easter Sunday, 20/20, there are 17 million Americans unemployed! There are double lines of cars across the nation, waiting to get food! Sometimes, there's no food left!

We are a First World country in the twenty-first century?

Trust me. I'm not 'chicken little,' but when our first grade teacher asked the class: "How do you think the farmer responded to 'chicken little?"
Our classmate, who lacked any inkling of couth, responded: He probably said: "Holy SH..! We got a talkn' chicken here!"

For the last hundred years or more, our country WAS not only free, but the wealthiest, the greatest, the most powerful, the most productive, and the best economy in the entire world.

Sadly today, our relationship with the rest of the world has reached the depths of being a virtual 'Little Orphan Annie.'
Where is daddy Warbucks now?
Where is 'Our Conductor?'
What page (s) are we on?

We cannot produce enough equipment and materials, to fight this virus. People are dying every day from the lack of equipment to fight back!

As of today, April 13, 20/20, the USA has 22,000 deaths! The State of New York has 10,000! The United States has more deaths from this virus, than any of the other #151 countries in the entire world!

Today, 4/12/2020, it was stated that ONLY the president could decide which states would 're-open' the economy.

Today, 4/16/2020, it will be up to each governor when they can re-open the economy?

Our leaders suggested that the protesters should help 'Liberate' three states; Michigan, Minnesota, and West Virginia!

Today, it was stated that we, the USA, had the least deaths from C-19 than all of the other #184 countries of the world! *(Where did those additional 33 countries come from? From three days ago? It was #151 then?) Factually, records show we have more deaths than any country in the world!* This is not nitpicking, it's calling out loose "canon-ism"! (if that's such a word).
The economy is shut down!

It appears that it can't get any worse than this?

The entire country is 'frozen' in time! Our alleged 'leaders' are failing in the management, and strategies, fighting this crisis.

Most of the previous comments were aimed at the millennial's generation. They are next in line for the baton.

Here is the challenge for the millennials to be the best generation EVER!

IF? They can get this country back to normality, and solemnity, we'll gracefully and gratefully pass the torch on to their generation.

You can pick and choose bits and pieces from our generation to help you. Good Luck, may God bless all of you! You'll need it.

"EXTRA-EXTRA. *Read all about it!*"

"Attention Mr. and Mrs. North and South America! And all the ships at sea!" Anybody know who used to say that?

It was Walter Winchell! The most popular newspaper and radio journalist during 1930's- 70's. That was his mantra coming on the air. Then he would say: 'Breaking News!'

Mostly about wars going on. You might be thinking? Who gives a rat's hind? Here's why.

Using his mantra, hope he don't mind? This is not 'Breaking news!' Just a heads up! When our Greatest Generation was flourishing, the 'swamp' was ebbing and flowing, with the good ol' boys lying on the beaches, enjoying the sun.

During these years, when we were going to grade school, grade school was co-ed.

Maybe? Some of us will want to join the 'good ol' boys on the beaches? Not so fast here.

By the time we graduated from grade school, we found out that the girls were one hell've lot smarter than we were! It was probative!

When we all entered into the worker's world, we quickly found out that 'the work forces' were co-ed, but not equal in pay! While working hip to hip performing the same duties?

Soon, the sun started shining through the crack's in the ceiling! ('chicken little' was right!) That same sun, was shining on the beaches of the swamp! Hey! The beaches should also be co-ed! Right!

Soon the ladies appeared! Slowly and surely, they started to share the same pebbles on the beaches, as the 'good ol' boys.'

Back in those days, there was a 'saying;' "You are NOT the only pebble on the beach, there's a 'Little Rock' in Arkansas!" Lo and behold, with the ladies on the beach, the tide started to change! Eventually, ladies were using more sun screen then the 'good ol' boys.'

Stocks busted through that crack in the ceiling for sun screen! Plus, the ladies were not only more attractive, but they are much smarter!

Hopefully, there will be more coming, who won't need the sun screen! History has already proven that sun screen is not a requisite for leadership!

OH! I'm sorry! I forgot! There will be an election in just a few months from now! "I forgot all about that !" For comparison of the generations: Here's a list of just a few of 'our' leaders.

Most Notables;
(Just the tip of the iceberg).

George H. W. Bush
Ronald Regan
Franklin Delano Roosevelt
Barack Obama
Muhammad Ali
Rosa Parks
Martin Luther King Jr.
Neil Armstrong
Buzz Adrian
Sally Ride
Jonas Salk
Robert Jarvic
Kleinert/Kutz
(and me)

Our G Gen 'members' are unending. They were our;

Role Models, Idols, Super Hero's, Patriots. They inspired us. We followed their lead. They were our conduit.

Publicly! Our leaders of the G Gen did not use backroom bar vulgar, nor grade school play ground slang.

They didn't slander their peers nor their counterparts. They didn't lie... *ALWAYS?*

I wonder? Are there ANY Idols, Super Hero's, Patriots…in today's generation? Can you identify any? Maybe that's our problems? None of the above? Our president George H W Bush is a chartered member of "The Greatest Generation."

His resume for 'membership' included his birth in the 1920's, survival of the Great Depression of 1929-33. World War ll. In addition, he was proactive in the Civil Rights movement. The Korean War, The Vietnam War, the Gulf Wars, and the conflicts in the Middle East, the later he served as The President of the United States.

He served in just about every level/capacity of politics ever known to mankind. One must wonder? How can any one man or one women, spend over fifty years in the political arena and survive without damaging, or mortal scars inflicted?

Based on today's culture, his canonization would be a 'Slam Dunk!'

In addition, he served during WW ll as a fighter pilot and cheated death numerous times, after being shot down, and rescued from the Pacific Ocean. Pause. By the way. Who did you say your idol's and hero's are?

Now. Hold on to those previous comments, and facts, and your 'thoughts' about them.

In the darkest days of the beginning of World War ll, sitting president (FDR), Franklin Delano Roosevelt, had 'fireside chats' with the United States of America, on the radio! No TV yet. Every radio in the neighborhood was on, and the volume was maxed out, for the entire neighborhood to hear.

"We" the people of the entire United States, could feel his arm draped around our shoulders with compassion, and empathy.

President Roosevelt talked to us as if we were sitting at his side, next to fire place. How soothing it felt to know everything would be ok. He promised us that we'd get through it. We **BELIEVED IN HIM!** AND! We did get through it, **TOGETHER!** He asked us to do our part, and warned us there would be indescribable sacrificing by all of us.

We accepted his challenge of: "OBEDIENCE," DISCIPLINE," "PATRIOTISM," Are these traits showcased anywhere today?

Our world was turned upside down, and sideways. But we stuck together. Because of wars, we were 'rationed' of every product that was produced, and was essential to our health. We excepted it. Unequivocally, our sacrificing was stretched to the limits. It would last for *FOUR* YEARS! Those sacrifices built character, and made us better, and a stronger individual.
It made us more 'appreciative' of all of the blessing that we had before the war. Isn't it ironic, that we don't know how good we have it, until we loose it?

History dictates that our generation spent over *TWENTY-FOUR* years at war! Plus three years of 'Great' depression.

Those twenty-four years of war, does not include all of the Middle East wars!

On the brighter side of today'sgeneration, the 'war' with COVID 19, is projected to last for *EIGHTEEN MONTHS AT THE LONGEST!* (LOOK! 'Is that tumbleweed bouncing and twirling in the wind' 'Again'?) *Pause, and ponder here.*

As I stated, we don't know how good we have it, until it is taken away from us. Today they call it 'Distancing.'

Previous to COVID-19, how many times did we want to hug each other, shake other's hands, say something nice about them, while pecking on their cheek?

After we get back to a normal life, let's all promise each other, that we will bring that style of life back again. Make the 'old norm' as the new norm.

For sure; No more regrets EVER! For NOT doing it in the new norm.
Today's Gen, has had only one other major crisis, that was inflicted on them. The unfathomable 9-11!! OOPS! I forgot about 9-11. There were many ***"Hero's"*** that came out of that one! Sorry about that.

We will have to let the historians decide which 'crisis' ' was the most devastating of all! Course, our generation witnessed the 9-11 also. I still don't know which was the most crucial of all. I do "Remember Pearl Harbor!" I was twelve years old. To us, it was Dooms Day! "Game Over!"

On the flip side, there will be good that will come out of this present pandemic, hopefully, it will open the doors to change our political structure, and our healthcare systems, that are an 'everlasting war' within the ranks. Life will get back to normal at a very heavy cost financially, humanly, with many deposits of scar-tissue.

Firstly, we must change our way of choosing our leaders. In my ninety-one years on this earth, I have never seen leaders of our country be so divisive. Our leaders are suppose to set examples for us.

I am blessed with the fact that I have lived during the terms of 13 presidents. From FDR, to Obama. During those 13 president's terms, there were:

The Great Depression… it lasted for three years.

WW ll...followed eight years later, and lasted four years.

Before we could take a good deep breath:
The Korean War…followed five years later, lasted three years.

Breathing was normal when:
The Vietnam War…followed, and lasted seventeen years!
The civil Rights Movement crisis started and ended during the Vietnam wars!

Breathing was rapidly changing, chests were filling like a hot air balloon! Pains escalated. There was no EMS, nor 911? Not even in our dreams. How in this world, did "WE" ever get through all of those crisis.' Is that 'why' we are 'The Greatest Generation?' Not bragging here, just proud as hell!

I have searched the archives of all of those 13 president's speeches: State of the Union Addresses, News, and press conferences etc. I could not find, NOT ONE of those documents had; "I" did this, "I" did that.

They all used the word "WE." Is that part of the reason why we are divided? Today?

Every one of those disasters, during my generation brought the entire country, and the world back together again. Did we make it look too easy… when we overcame everyone of those disasters…with unity, sacrifices, obedience, and discipline, that lasted FOREVER!

Emphasizing "FOREVER!" Our (Greatest) generation is still unified; respectable, courteous, loving, carrying, sincere, honest, obedient, discipline. Yes, every one of the above!

As stated, the 9-11 crisis, and today's, COVID-19, are only two crisis to hit the millennials!

How will they respond to them? Only history will tell how they handled their crisis. Sometimes I believe I can speak for my generation, that 'today's' generation bans together, during, and shortly thereafter a crisis, but when the dust settles, it's back up on the horse again. No pain, no foul!

"Drinks on the house!" "Set em' up in the next alley!"

That might sound a little hurtful? But, here's where I am going with this.

We, my generation, believes that not only the millennia's, but the twenty-first generationeers, are lacking the depth of the 'sensitivity' neuron that we had, and still have.

Example here: After seventy five years! We still honor and recognize all of the 400,000 soldiers who lost their lives during WW ll only.

In retrospect to the above, how many cars do you see in a cemetery in your own home town on a Sunday afternoon?

During our generation, EVERY cemetery was bumper to bumper with cars. The 'crowd' size was likened to that of Woodstock."

Our dad would take us there every Sunday afternoon! That was a 'treat' for us.

In today's world, you see cars bumper to bumper, with families paying respect to their members, until the fresh flowers die off. Then, it's nearly a ghost town on Sunday afternoons.

We all know why it's a ghost town. Dare, we'll be there when the flowers are still fresh?

If you ask every person, who served, and is serving our country, we all feel the same about "Patriotism." When you wear any one of the uniforms of the armed forces, of The United States of America, that uniform is a wellspring of patriotism that flows from head to toe: FOR THE REST OF YOUR LIFE! That patriotism is built with discipline, obedience, and commitment. Those fourteen weeks of basic training, during wartime, instills a camaraderie that is beyond recall. In your minds eye, you are guaranteed that your buddy has your back and you have his. And we'd lay our life down for each other.

Being brutally honest, and frank, I believe that our millennials do not have those tools on their belts. I believe that modern technology, has affected (diminished) the level of *Virtue ness* of our Generation.

Thankfully, there are no wars going on. No need for drafting individuals to protect our country as we had, to create our level of "Patriotism."
I often wonder? How will historians profile the leaders of this generation? Will the millennial's be as proud, and respectful, as we still are of loosing love ones? After seventy-five years!

Today, the core of our political leaders could be infected by a 'virus' that could be spreading into the bowels of our political leaders of our country?

The more than 400 alleged leaders in (DC), the epic center of the most damaging '*VIRUS*' of inhumane treatment, since the discovery of America.

Numerous polls of the American people, says that our country has fallen into such a disarray morally, like never before!

My generation had never witnessed the following pathetic, and most disgusting actions of both political parties of the 21st century.

Never did the Speaker of the House tear up a document of the State of The Union address by the president of the United States! On National (world) TV!

Never did a president of the United States EVER fail to shake hands with the Speaker of The House, when it was offered…ON national TV!

Remember! These are OUR "LEADERS" of a free and First World country!
Let's wash our hands here for twenty seconds, and let politics go down the drain.

Re-COVID-19. We are quarantined in our own homes, with, and without our entire families! Can you even fathom the pressure of anxiety, stress, and the squabbling between the children, and mom and dad!
Maybe, it has also affected the legislature in the same manner?
The social medium is filled with 'help measures' to deal with mental pressures.

This pandemic will leave a trail of mentally disordered human beings, who will exceed the present and past vets with (PTSD).

Today's social medium provides help with every E-Gad known to mankind for PTSD victims.

On a personal note, I think to myself? *MANY* "Help" suggestions are common sense!

Our generation never had the social medium to help us, common sense was inherent. Our 'mentality' was immunize
Our generation's 'social medium' was the radio, and the newspaper only! Can any of the millennials even fathom that?
With no doubt in anyone's mind, in my 91 years on this earth, there was never such a tragedy as this COVID-19! Then add the political environment, are not only Game changers? They are World changers! We all must be stronger than ever before. So, why was our fight for life during my generation inherent? Here's one of many whys.

Most of my generation was born in or near the 'great' depression.
Because of the systemic of depression, it drove many husbands and fathers to alcoholism.

Mom's were stay-at-home moms. Our parents argued incessantly. Mainly, at bedtime. We laid awake EVERY night, wondering when it would turn physical! Some nights it did. Two of us slept in that same bedroom, and the other two were in the adjacent bedroom.
It was like that from the cradle to marriage! OVER *TWENTY-YEARS!* I was the last one to get married, just a month before my 22nd birthday.

Like the political arena, pre C-19, my family, and many other families, were 'damaged goods' from the time our unbiblical-cord was pinched off.

"Obedience" and "Discipline" were maxed out, for all of us!

Aside: For all of you recovering alcoholics, who are attending meetings, and all al anons. We loved our dad! He probably spent 95% of his time drinking or hung-over. But! that remaining 5% was spent with us on EVERY Sunday afternoon. *(The only time he was sober)*. Yes, we went to the cemetery!

To this day, we have more indelible memories from that 5%, than we do of those 95% times. In addition, here's one of them.

Every year dad would play Santa Claus for our neighbor's kids. Unfortunately, since most fathers were drinkers, each time our dad (as Santa) made a visit, he was greeted with a cocktail! Some times it was a straight shooter of Old Grand Dad! After spreading good cheer to the neighbors, by the time that his sleigh landed back to our backyard, he was pretty well 'out of it.' We'd have to help him get out of the sleigh, roll him in the house to his bed, get him out of his red suit. Help him get into his 'trap door' p.j's. Before we got the covers over him, he was 'out like light.'

Since we were so poor, we couldn't afford to buy a regular Christmas tree. (Add this to that 5% portion that he gave us).

He'd take us with him, to buy a Christmas tree. In the very back of the lot, there were trees that looked like they got ran over by an eighteen wheeler. Because of it's condition, the cost of it was drastically discounted!

We had a small pot belly coal stove that kept the entire house warm. He would take the poker, you might not know what a 'poker' is or was? It is a straight wrought iron rod, with a handle on it. When the big lumps of coal were burning down, you would poke it to break it apart to re-ignite itself, to keep the heat on a steady flow. Dad would stick that poker inside the door of the stove to get the point of it as hot as hell's fire! Where there was an opening in the tree, (a branch missing, probably still dragging under that eighteen wheeler) he'd burn a hole in the shaft of the tree. Then cut another branch off, from a dense area, and stick it in that newly burned hole.

All four of us brothers are taking that smell of pine, it was always a pine tree, and that burning of that tree, to our graves. All of the money in the world couldn't buy those memories that he spent with us at Christmas time.

On the other side of that coin, and thankfully, most of those bad nights between mom and dad, have faded off into the sunset.

However, this one Christmas, our ages were about four to eight years old, we were really having a good time playing with our toys and hollering and laughing. Of course ol' "Santa" was asleep and snoring out loud, and dead to the world!

Back in those days, if one light burned out of a set of eight or ten, the entire set didn't work. It was a guessing game of which light burnt out?

Lo and behold, while dad was in bed soundly asleep, we kids were attempting to find out which light was burnt out.

Because of his revamped tree, it caught on fire and it quickly spread through the house! We laughed that much louder! Mom screamed out: "Be quiet! You might wake him up!"

I am sure there are many other spouses of alcoholics, who might feel that same way?

To this day, my three brothers and I still use the same method of the handling of arguing and fighting between siblings. I'd like to share that with you.

I assume, because of our living conditions, from the cradle to wedding, we became immune to incidents that were upsetting us.

We never had a quarrel between any of us! During our pre, and teen years, adulthood, and even to this today, here's our method of solidarity: Whenever, a conversation between us started going sideways, one of us would blare out! "How 'bout' dem Cubs?" Meaning; drop this conversation now! Whether that conversation was about politics, religion, or personal opinion, it evaporated. It was deleted! We respected, and honored each other's convictions. As you'll see, we developed many more method's of solidarity as a family and country.

I will also be brutally honest and frank about my convictions. Honesty and frankness are not popular. Nobody likes 'Frank' anyway, but that's the way it is.

Please forgive me when I 'brag' too much about my generation, my literary choice of words are limited. Sort of like our leader. Of course, I blame it on having only nine years of formal education. I don't know what his problem is?

Sister Hilda was my teacher in the eight grade. She'd bang my head against that chalkboard every day! For not knowing English, spelling and grammar. I graduated with a 47 percentile in all categories! True story!
 SEE! Frank's here!

But! If you lived during our generation, you would be just as proud. It is your chance for chest bumping and high fives…IF you can get us back to normality.

Virtual this: (the word 'virtual' was reinvigorated since C-19).

Your generation is in the 'batter's box.' It's your time to display; "Obedience" and "Discipline."

I guarantee you this: *(In our times, there were no cameras out in the center field stands relaying the pitches by the catcher, to our manager in the dugout!)*

Hopefully, you will attempt to follow some of the reasons for our bragging.

I am a Catholic. (Not bragging here, nor playing the religious card).
I believe that God does not punish us for sinning. He forgives us for our sins.

However, I don't know if the Catholic Church agrees with me here, but I believe that God lets things happen, to warn us about sinfulness, in today's world.

I believe that we were given a 'warning' pre-COVID-19, when our country started going to hell in a hand basket. Namely, when the present leaders took over! Down deep in my heart, I thought we'd come together sooner than later. But, not so.

Maybe? God is letting this virus be our strike two? By letting it spread world wide?

If I am correct in my crystal balling, this could be the bottom of the ninth inning with the game tided?

With two outs, and 3&2 on the batter.

"GAME OVER!"

Don't YOU snicker or make fun of my prediction. I won't be here but YOU might?

The Greatest Generation
(FYI, my personal life)

I was born on February 6, <u>1929!</u> The year is underscored, due to it's significance in my life. Explanation to follow.

I grew into to a lanky teenager by my thirteen birthday. I weighed 175 lbs. and 6' 4" tall. That was considered tall back in the 30's/40's. My legs were longer than normal. Making my torso shorter than most. I was aptly dubbed by my peers as; "High Ass."

I was self-conscious, and had a bottomed out low esteem of my over all stature, and myself. I lived six house away from our hang out, 'safe place,' a sweet shop; candy and ice cream store. In my minds eye; walking past those six houses, every 'old lady,' on both sides of the street, were peeking out from behind their curtains, laughing at me! Thinking: "There's that dirty ol' Kleier boy, they can't afford a haircut. Plus his ass is way too high!" Being brutally honest, I did look a like "Kramer" (Seinfeld). We didn't have enough money for a regularly scheduled haircut.

(That's me as 'Kramer' in my back yard 1947) WWWOOOHHH! No wonder I had such a low esteem of myself! Note also, my 'high ass'! Frank's back!

My 'formal' education: One year of high school.

I was thrust into sub-poverty living conditions from birth. At the age of fifteen, it was mandatory that I seek employment to put food on the table for the family. Inheritably, my families educational standards dictated only one year of high school would be max.

> *Aside: This year, 2020, just about every prom, and graduation ceremony were cancelled due to COVID-19. Many of the students showed much sorrow and brokenhearted ness, knowing that they spent four years of high school, or even college, and wont be able to experience those activities. My heart sincerely goes out to all of them. That had to be devastating to them.*
>
> *I'm caught in a catch-22 again. I don't know what words to use here either. But, I am being honest and frank. My three brother's and I, were like many families during our generation, our parents couldn't afford to pay for our education.*
> *The pastor of our grade school told everybody who couldn't afford to go to a catholic high school, to come see him, and he'd work out a discounted payment plan. Tuition back then was $300.00 a year. He worked out a deal for $5.00 a month for mom and dad. That's*

$45.00 a year! Mom would give us a $5.00 bill once a month. We'd take it to the office and get a receipt. Due to dad's drinking habit, there were times when mom didn't have the $5.00! When it was due, we never went to the office.

The good brother would run us down out in the school yard during recess, and ask us; "Where the money"? We told him mom didn't have it. He told us to tell her that is not acceptable! You see! He was also brutally honest and frank!

*Soon we got so far behind, that they turned it over to a collection agency! Remember now, all four of us were about two years apart in age, so, just one of us would go there every two years. Mom couldn't afford $45.00 every other year! WE **WERE** IN THE **Minority**! Eventually dad had to take bankruptcy for the second time. FYI. The tuition for this same school, is now $17,000.00*

Therefore, we knew when we graduated from grade school, we only had one year of education left, our freshmen year in high school. We all had to get a job. In fact, my high school teacher, a brother, told us to take our books home, but come back tomorrow for our final tests. He didn't know it, but we always had to walk to school…or walk home from school. When he said that, I started running, and was almost airborne when I reached the alleyway that we normally used to walk to or from school!. I never went back the next day to even take our tests. I knew I wouldn't be going back next year.

Here's how poor we were! We had a choice to ride a trolley, to or from school. Mom would buy car-checks they called them, (street-cars) a token to get on the street-car. The car-checks cost $0.15 for two of them. Mom told us that we could ride only one way…to school…or from school! Mostly, we rode to school.
We lived on the city limit line. The school was down town, about a three mile walk.

The reason for playing the 'poverty card' was, proms and graduation were NEVER even an option for us, not even in our dreams. But, we accepted that gracefully.

In 1944, just one month after my fifteenth birthday…my dad swore under oath…a legal document…stating that I was sixteen years old, so I could drive a truck. Even today! My drivers license shows I was born in 1928, making me ninety-two years old! In reality, I **AM** *'only'* **ninety -one** years old. My birth certificate plainly shows that I was born in 1929. Can you imagine how many times I had to sign legal documents, loans, bank statements, etc…and showed my ID! FOR 76 YEARS! Most of all, I was drafted in the army in 1951! Still, absolutely **NOBODY** has ever noticed the difference in my date of birth? Kind of scary in a way, isn't it?

I am the author of multi books about my family growing up in poverty. Humbly, and finally, one of my books landed on the shelf in the Archives at Nordstrom Library, at the University of Louisville, and also the Louisville Free Public Library. My mantra: "If you must shovel SH.. for a living…be the best damn SH—shoveler in the entire world." My Dad passed that advice on to us. Because horse and wagons were still on the streets! Someone from the city would have to shovel up their poop. Obviously, it was the lowest paying job in the city.

My birth, which was in the first trimester of the "Great Depression," was destined for stormy weather, and rocky roads.

Entering the man's work force at the age of fourteen, after I just completed my first year of high school, my resume did not have train-like letters following my name. However, my many years of serving public entrepreneurs, for the first twenty-plus years of my life in the work force, I proudly graduated with a 'Masters' in "Street Sense:" summa cum laude! This assessment (Street Sense) was passed onto me from my grand-paw, who was a life-time professional carpenter. On my very first day in high school, because of my height, the teacher, a 'Brother' (Catholic) high school, all boys, said: "Anyone wanting to play basketball stand up!"

A few stood up. He then said: "STAND UP KLEIER!" (because of my height) I stood up, but never went to the gym to practice. He didn't know that I was clumsier than a clown with my "High Ass,' and my severe case of an inferiority complex. Plus I still looked like "Kramer."

I'm very proud to announce that my grand-paw's philosophy and advice about "Street Sense," came thirty years before "Sesame Streets" debut on TV, and eighty years before that movie! Let me gloat here a minute… along with all of my other piers, and *"generationeers"!* "Street Sense" was not only prevalent, but it was our culture. A full formal education was as scarce as a hen's tooth. Our mom always told us: "All of us 'uneducated' are "Ignorant of the facts!" Meaning: Their parents never discussed social anthropology, health, politics, more importantly, biology with them. Our parents trended their parents. And, so did our grade school teachers. SO! We *really* were 'ignorant of the facts,' as mom said.

We were clueless about marriage, childbirth, and the dreaded word "SEX," until we were teenagers! Sadly, we learned all about the 'real world' from gutter talk, or "Street Sense." The later; The good the bad and the ugly.

Can you believe this? At the time of these writings, 'they' are proposing a sex-ed for K grades! This is one of the many reasons that I am publishing this book.

Drastic changes, since we were kids. As budding teenagers, we never used the word SEX! Didn't even know what it meant. We didn't know where babies came from, or how they were made! Sex-ed in K grades! Mom's are letting their four year olds listen to the babies heart beat in their belly! WOW! Call 911, my generation is floored! Can't Breath!

My focus, is on every generation still living, moreover, "The Millennials" and "The Gen X's." "They" are the ones who will be running this country in just a few short years.

I want them to try to compare our life style and culture to theirs, since we were deemed: "The Greatest Generation." Hopefully, they can pick up a few pointers that could help them.

My generation of moms and dad's formal education, and their piers, maxed out at the fifth grade. Their resume showed (Cropper) farm worker. They also had to seek jobs early in life, for family survival.

"Scholastically," we followed their trend. But we extended our education status past our parents. We were able to get one year of high school under our belts. (No back packs back then, we used dad's old pant belts to carry our books to school).

All of us, (no sisters) my three brothers and me, because of our age, would turn fourteen at the end of our first year of high school. It was inevitable, our first job would be a man's job. The law stated that we had to apply for a "Work Permit" at the county office. (No child labor laws back then! Many places never had a time clock, or a time card!)

Needless to say, our family wasn't the only family faced with these problems. It was the culture at that time, which was the staple and core of why we were aptly named: The "Greatest Generation!" So, put a check mark in that box.

Our grand-paw, my mom's dad, was well aware of our financial status, knowing we would never be able to attend four years of high school. As you'll see, he was right! Not only about formal education, but also about "Street Sense." "Thanks grand-paw." Just remember, he has approximately fifty plus years of 'wisdom' under his belt! He will share it with you. Take advantage of it. It's a free course in "Street Sense." Grand-paw's close relationships are more effective, and meaningful to you, because of his status in life: Non-working, retired No shopping! Free of obligations. No commitments of any kind. One hundred percent concentration on you, and his love for you is unfathomable. Just remember, he is paying forward. You will too.

Caveat: Millennials! Today's Statistics, pre C-19, show that adults between the ages of 19-28…are most likely to be scammed! So, listen, read, and educate yourselves, when deciding major investments financially, or in your own life's goals. All of us have regrets, but let's try to mitigate them. _

I highly recommend that you slip your feet into my shoes when attempting to compare my culture to yours. See if you can feel how I felt, but, the back story here, could you have done what we did? Or how would you have done it differently than we did. Moreover, what will you do to change your culture and generation for your descendents?

Trust me, here. I'm trying to convey our 'culture' to you, for only one purpose, that is, so you will know how we lived. We do not expect any generation to live like we did, except for the virtues that we possessed.

Challenges? for going down in history as being the: "Greatest" Generation EVER!

Don't even entertain the possibility of not being the greatest. You must strive for being the best at anything you do.

Firstly: The restoration of: "Obedience" "Discipline" "Patriotism" and above all, "Loving our Neighbor," must take place.

Flash back: On my very first job, a man's job, at the age of fifteen, our boss implemented a program headed, "ZERO DEFECTS." We all raised our eyebrows and rolled our eyes as if he was playing without a full deck. Our job was servicing customers with towels, aprons, bed linens and uniforms.

His office was across from the lobby of the plant. He could see us come in to work, and also when we left for the day. The norm was, that we'd wave goodbye to him, to let him know we were leaving. However, if he didn't wave goodbye to you, he'd wave to you, to come to his office! That wave sent 'chills' up and down your spine, because you knew that you 'screwed up' somewhere! Instead of meeting with your buddies at the nearest 'watering hole,' which was also the norm, you were going to be late getting there.

We would have never dreamed in our lifetime, how close we came to having "Zero Defects!" Only because we dreaded that 'wave' to come to his office, and being late getting to our buddies.

He proved to us, that he knew that we'd never have 'Zero Defects,' but we came pretty damn close to it. Those waves from him to come to his office, drastically decreased. And, our gathering at the water hole was much more enjoyable.

More on Zero Defects later.

Preface

The bible tells us about the shepherd who left 99 of his flock, to set out to find the 'lost *ONE*.' Let's put this into perspective.

Envision this scenario in today's world. Let's reverse that script. THEE ninety-nine are lost! Not the one! THEE ninety-nine cannot hear today's shepherd's voice!

It sounds like a clanging bell or a cymbal to them! Nothing but revenge, anger, hate, hostility, maliciousness is spewing all over, not only in our countryside but the entire climate of the world. "We **WERE**, the shepherd of the world!"

The biblical shepherd was very conscientious about EVERY one of his sheep. He knew they were a bunch of dumb asses. But he loved them and cared about their livelihood. Painstakingly, he would navigate them to the most flourishing areas for pasturing. 'They' claim that the biblical shepherd knew each one of them personally. He even gave them names! Evidently, they really did recognize his voice. Let's attempt to compare the biblical shepherd, that is, the one's with 'boots on the ground' shepherd.

The "alleged" shepherd's of this 21st Century…also, the ones with boots on the ground, don't understand what's in The Constitution of The United States of America! Both sides of the isle decipher it differently! OH! I know why! The Framers culture was different 276 years ago! DUH! TWO DUHS! Why hasn't that been updated before now? Can you even imagine that "DUELING" is still in it!

Today's alleged shepherds don't know right from wrong! They justify it! How can they take care of the ninety-nine lost, when they have no respect for each other? Good luck Millennials! You will really need more than luck. You might want to start looking skyward for that shoeless Shepherd! HE will be your salvation.

Did you know that we all have a very tiny cell, it's itty-bitty, in our brain? It's called 'a mirror neuron.' Sometimes it ignites immediately when we come in contact with other human beings, sometimes it's dim, not very clear, but other times it's liken to an approaching hurricane. These neurons then prompt us to imitate whomever we are with. When we see someone happy, or sad, or angry, our mirror appears. We want to share that person's feelings and thoughts with them. After all, we human beings are; 'the most imitative of all living creatures.' Yes, even more than monkeys. *Maybe, we all want to be role models.*"

I bet you're thinking; "This guy has more than "Street Sense," he must be a brain surgeon! He knows all about 'neurons.' "

NO! I'm just a dirty old truck driver who delivered linens and uniforms to every active business, including brothels! We were cast in the same category as the dumb ass sheep. This job was 'almost' the dirties job for all of us 'uneducated' people. It's imperative that I'm explicit in telling you why I was a dirty ol' truck driver, and the reason for my low esteem.
When I entered a place of business, the owners, and workers would yell out: "Here's the dirty ol' towel man! Get all of the dirty towels together for him!" That alone will make you very humble.

My job was to go into the establishments, and yes even the brothels, and count each piece of dirty linens and towels etc, with my bare fingers and hands. Let's say we counted fifty dirty towels, ten dirty bed sheets, etc… We'd bag them up and throw them up on top of the truck.

Shooting those bags of dirty linens on top of the truck, (similar to taking a jump shot in basketball) was to separate the dirty linens from the clean ones, for decontamination purposes.

(Taking my lunch break @ my house 1947, in the 1939 GMC truck.)

HOWEVER! That being said, listen to this system of even exchange function: "A clean article for each dirty one counted." We'd enter the cargo door to the fresh clean linens. We counted out fifty clean towels, and ten clean sheets, with the same 'bacterium' on our hands and fingers from counting the dirty ones, and yes, even out of the brothel! Yucky pooh-pooh!

The clean linens were tied up numerically, based on the size of the linens. That is, bed sheets were tied in bundles of ten. Bath towels twenty-five etc…by a string only! Not wrapped in plastic, or paper, as they are today. So, we had to touch *EACH* piece of clean linen with our contaminated hands and fingers.

I hope you got a strong stomach. We also had to service the University's dental college. They had hundreds of bloody linen neck napkins. (No paper ones at these times). You know the drill! Each dirty one was touched first.

The upscale restaurants had bins or bags in their storage room for their dirty linens. In the hot summer months, maggots and roaches were rampant.
Yep! We touched those same clean napkins with our unsanitary fingers. It was incomprehensible to wash our hands each time we touched the dirty stuff. I apologize for being so graphic, but that's another piece of the puzzle why we were the G Gen. How many of you millennials would do that job today?

These types of conditions made us a stronger person. (*We didn't mind getting our hands dirty!*) It made us very humble.

It was just another tool to better ourselves, and build character. In doing so, we helped in changing a better life for this generation. (On the other side of the coin, in relations to diseases, I'm ninety-one years old, in pretty good health. Did I grow a pretty strong immune system by being exposed to those conditions?) Could I have survived COVID-19? Back to the mirror neuron. I do have one. You better have it, when dealing with the public 24/7.

My dad always told us; "If you must shovel sh.. for a living, be the best sh… shoverler in the world. I felt the same about being a linen delivery guy. I wanted to be the best in the whole world, it also applies to any occupation, career, or profession.

My Goal in life? It is the same today, as it was 76 years ago; be the best I can at doing anything! When I got into that truck for the very first time, and released that steel emergency hand-brake, it came up through the floor board, just like the steel gear shift did. That hand brake had a squeeze handle on it. You'd pull it back squeezed, then release your squeeze when it was secured. That was our 'parked' gear! The gear shift was in neutral. If you didn't put that hand brake in the right place, the truck would roll away when you got out of it. I turned the key on, and with the engine running, I'd push down on the regular steel brake pedal, (no pad on it) with my right foot, holding it firmly down. With my left foot, I push down on the steel clutch, (no pad on that either) completely to the floor board, with my right hand I insert the steel gear stick on the floor, into the first gear slot on that 1939 GMC truck. I slowly eased the clutch upward with my left foot, I remove my right foot from the brake pedal, release the hand brake, move my right foot to the gas pedal, and then slowly mash it to the floor. Now I'm off and running. Reaching speeds of 35 MPH! I was flying! Daytona! Here I come!

For those of you whom have never driven a stick gear on the floor, you had to get up to a certain speed, before you could shift the gear into second gear, and the same for shifting into the third gear. You couldn't skip any gear! If you did, the motor would shut down.

(Hey Millennials! Can you even fathom doing that? SWITCHING GEARS! EVERY TWO OR THREE TRAFFIC LIGHTS! DOWN TOWN! Today, they would call those five functions; "Distracted driving"! That was five functions for us. You guys have only two! If that?

Is your mirror 'neuron' on? You guys will soon be able to get into your car in New York, **and by your voice;** the door opens, the engine starts up, your GPS turns on.

Then you hop in the back seat and wake up in LA! Just think about that! How far you guys are past my lifetime! Do you ever think about what it will be like when you are ninety-one years old? Again, we helped you to be able to make that trip to LA. That's why we were here, so you guys could figure out a better way of life, than ours. We weren't hero's or some kind of savior, it was our duty. You will do the same as we did. We hope and pray.

Back to the ancient times, driving that 1939 GMC truck. When our boss told us that he was going to implement a program for 'customer service' called; ZERO DEFECTS, all of our mirror neurons swirled. Like a hurricane! We all rolled our eyes quickly. We thought this guy is sick, or he needs a psychiatrist!

Well! Lo and behold, in a short period of time, he 'sold' us on his program. He became our role model! We wanted to imitate him. We soon learned from him, that we had to put our hearts and souls in it with grim determination, to have ZERO DEFECTS.

If you don't want to give anything you want to do, 100%? Forget about it, give it up, don't waste your time.

He knew, and we all knew, that there could never be ZERO DEFECTS, but we have to strive for that. If you have never strived for perfection, you don't know what you're missing. That feeling is beyond recall. You must push yourself to the limit when setting goals, whether it be a diet, breaking a habit, making the team, getting that promotion, winning a trophy. Just strive for it, the road to perfection in it's self, is unfathomable!

'They" say that he who has gratification will get more, and those who have less gratification will receive less! Seems like one heck of a deal to me! In retrospect, even though this is a 'personal' feeling for me, I feel like I am just a reflection of our generation. That's the way it was.

Aside. My very first boss, was more of a father to me than my own dad, my dad was an alcoholic, my boss taught me how to handle the roller coaster of life.

When we attempt to prove certain phenomenon's, such as…the 'greatest,' and the 'worst' EVER, it is virtually impossible to comprehend the differentials. However, there is an advantage, if you were blessed with living through two or three generations.

So bear with me in my attempt to shed enlightenment on the object of perception. Especially when comparing generations in the past, to the present, and projecting the life style of the future.

A 'line' (agreed on) created mentally, shouldn't be crossed. Unfortunately, some 'lines' are marked in the sand, which can easily be brushed over with our bare foot, and erase it, leaving no boundaries.

I will provide sufficient probative evidence for you. But for sure! You will NOT get second hand information, 'he said she said,' you'll get it straight from the horses mouth.

Rest assured; The overwhelming comments, statistics, suggestions, constructive criticism, predictions, are based on twenty plus years of associated members of; Physical therapy, fitness center gaurs, assisted living centers, golf foursomes. Our average age is 85 years old. The stats presented are unanimously agreed upon. Most likely universally. Wisdom is filling the air. I am blessed to live as long as I have, and have the privilege of being able to witness these times in person, and share them with you.

In addition, I have also gained specs of wisdom from the past generation, as well as the present generation. The wisdom gained during these generations are unfathomable to say the least. I'm still a dumb ass, but the wisdom that I have gained trumps that. I hope you can gain just half as much wisdom as I have. You'll be the happiest person in the world. Just follow your heart, and be honest.

When we judge others, we will also be judged. PLEASE! PLEASE! Do not take my bragging as being vain! I'm just trying to share my pleasures, and my blessings, with you, in hopes you will be able to do the same.

If you are old enough to remember the TV series, "Dragnet," the star of the show, Jack Webb, (Joe Friday's) mantra: "Just the facts m'am!" If you're not that old, just ask: "Echo," "Alexis," Etc…So, here are the facts. However, when you use Echo and Alexis, your neurons are soundly sleeping! Please keep your neurons awake 24/7.

Chapter 1

(Defining…lines)

"These are The facts ma'am."

To compare our generations, this 'manuscript' could also be labeled Documental, Journalistic, Self-help? Humor? Informative? Inspirational? And, some very good stories.

Have you ever seen maybe one word, one phase, one paragraph, one story…in writing, that made "YOUR" light shine? Maybe it hit your desire 'neuron'? It tells you: ***"THAT!" is what I want to do!"*** If that's the case, than you must strive for excellence! It won't be easy, as my dad said: "Put your nose to the grindstone!"

My grand-paw would come out to our house every Tuesday night (1930/40's), with two of his adult sons, to play Pinochle with our dad. When they came in the door, he and our two uncles would greet us all, warmly, attentively, and respectably. (I-phones, I-pads, 'Tweeters" etc. were not even on the drawing board). My brother Jerry, and I were six, and four years old, respectively. Grand-paw's philosophy, and the culture during these times, was; "Kids should be seen and not heard!" We accepted that ideology, as we did with any and all other system of social beliefs. Especially; *discipline.* You did not question it. It was the culture.

You did what you were told. If you didn't, you would suffer the '*Consequences*.' Trust me, 'consequences back then' was NOT: 'Time out,' OR, 'Sitting in the corner,' for a period of time, or taking your phone or I-pod, away from you for a short period of time.

In retrospect, our uneducated generation was smart enough to know that to '*Obey:*' The laws of the homestead (parent's rules), our teacher's rules, and governmental laws…would be *"Pain-Free!"* To obey, was just plain ol' common "Street Sense." To obey, should also apply today. And yes, it is still *"Pain-Free!"* It can save your life! Back to grand-paw's card game.

As always, here's the way we handled 'kids should be seen not heard' syndrome. We made a game out of it.

Brother Jerry and I sat on the floor, with our backs leaning against the wall. Our living room was so small, our legs were on the floor, under their chairs!

With our lips zipped! With a #2 pencil, and scraps from our tablet, we wrote notes to each other, poking fun at their conversations! We had more fun than they did playing cards.

Flash forward here, 2020 politics, defining lines. Senator John McCain lll, who served our country for 32 years in the senate, plus six years in Vietnam, where he was shot down in Hanoi, and suffered brutal torture while in solitary confinement.

Because of incessant complication's with health issues, mainly brain damage, sadly, he passed away August 25, 2018 while still active in office, serving our country.

Just a short seven months after his death, the sitting president has been very vocal, in berating senator McCain!

Partly, when asked why he didn't like McCain, his answer was, and I quote; *"I never did like him, and never will!" He never voted for a bill I wanted passed!"* Senator McCain was a poster for what America stands for…Patriotism, and gave his life for our country, and for you and me.

With those type of comments from a president of the United States of America, is just more proof, that we, the citizens of the United States of America are caught in the middle. Today's leaders remind me of my days in the fourth grade out in the school yard. And, it was bipartisan back then, and is now. It's a cancer that is spreading like wildfire! Both sides, are found ***"GUILTY AS CHARGED!"***

Let's switch gears here. Social medium, the sporting world, and politics, has turned our world upside down. There will be a severe consequence, if you do cross over an established and agreed upon line of rules and laws. #Caveat! (Be open minded).

"Get your heart on for Valentines Day!"

"If your penis is crooked or bent like a banana, we can correct that problem!" These quotes are advertisements for men's health clinics in the national/local newspapers! And! On TV! Call 9-1-1!

The graphics in print, and video, show two sets of bare legs, from under covers from knee to feet, the top set, toes down, bottom set, toes up. HUM! Can we 'decipher' what that really means? Now then, did I cross over the line here? Or, did the publishers and producers of advertising…print/TV? Or did we both, brush our foot over that line in the sand? I know one thing for sure! If my mom would have seen those adds in print or on TV, she and all of her peers in the United States of America would have swallowed their Adam's apple. How does your mom compare to ours? Our mom's world of morality and prudence, which was passed onto us kids, was unfathomable.

Even though that synopsis of the advertisements, which is of such a private and personal nature, it is just a flicker of what the future will hold for all of us in our country in regard to moral standards.

Flashback; the 1940's. Jane Russell, buxom star's movie; "Outlaw" was banned because she exposed; *too much cleavage!* Compare that to today's nearly-nude exposure of body parts. Are you following me here?

Prudence and morality, as we knew it, will NEVER return to this world. No matter how long you live! Unless You millennials do win out, being the best gen EVER! Our Gen saw the world through our lenses, as you baby boomers, millennials and gen Xs are seeing the world through your lenses.

What is so crucial about these, and many other social media promos are; what will those advertisements be like when those three generations reach maturity? Will those 'influencers' uncover full bodies?

Let's use the word 'influencer' as a thing; an object, namely the 'textor,' your e-gad that you actually 'text' your message on. Then we add; An influencee which is me, and the influencer, is you.

If you have used that 'object' as a device for pornography, defaming, degrading, to destroy another person's life, which that device entices us to hide behind, in a cowardly manner, the fabric of morality, prudence, self-esteem, and courtesy of this world, is deemed useless. A line must be drawn here! NOT in the sand!

My generation: NEVER did we see any football player hit another player on his bare head with a helmet.

NEVER did we see mob-like fights that cut a game short of the full sixty minutes of playing time of football, IN THE NFL! NEVER did we see a little league parents in mob-like fights during any games. NEVER did we see a youth basketball referee be assaulted…by parents… to the extent of bloody eyes and face.

NEVER did we see the entire football field, basketball court, covered with fans from both sides fighting for their lives.

NEVER did we see, security and law enforcement, for safety sakes, escort referees and coaches out of arenas.

Now, let's admit what my generation of sports did, that would be considered unsportsmanlike conduct…"compared" to *"Today's"* infractions, that could be classified as a misdemeanor, or a felony?

The "LINE in the sand:" Sports!

Believe this or not, my generation DID have television of sports…for about the past fifty-plus years of the over hundred years of sports, in modern history. We did have replays, highlights etc…being tactful here…we DID NOT have: UNPATRIOTIC demonstrations! When the National Anthem was played anywhere, we placed our hand over our heart, took our hats off, stood at attention, never blinked an eye, and the overwhelming majority of us, shed many tears…thinking of how many hero's wasn't here with us. And, silently, we thanked them from the bottom of our hearts, for letting us be here.

It is really unfortunate that I can't begin to describe, nor anyone else can, that very personal feeling of patriotism that my entire generation had when the National Anthem was played, and our flag flying!

That feeling was, and still is deep in our hearts. That will never change. Demonstrations will not change that! I'm sure that this generation's patriotism is very sincere to millions, but the depth of 'our' patriotism is immeasurable. In defense of this generation, and others, they never witnessed any major 'world wars.' Comprehending the depth of our patriotism, is incomprehensive able!

Wearing any one of the uniform's of the armed services of the USA, is indelible.

Let's ponder, and look into the future for what will the next generation be like? Will patriotism dwindle further down than the division of our country is now?

The following comments are made in good faith. We are not trying to belittle, cause shame, or attempt to show that we were saints, compared to today's generation. We had a few sinners, who were in the minority, among us.

The point here, someone has to take a good look at just how bad things are in today's world. Not only in politics and sports, but sexually, morally, religion, and socially. The whole ball of wax.

After searching through the archives of a myriad of films and videos of ALL of sports, we found only one incident that could be considered 'inappropriate' during our Gen.

A college coach was watching an opposing runner, speeding wide open near the sideline of the coaches bench, with the goal line in his cross hairs, inevitably for a touchdown! The coach physically tackled him to the ground! "Kill that coach, crucify him! That bad man!" Was that a misdemeanor or a felony? (PUN) The headlines on the next day's paper stated: "The WORST unsportsmanlike conduct in the history of the game!" SO, that was our worst ever.

Compare that to the previous infractions mentioned of today's gen. That's just a few snippets of why our generation was so much different then today's generation in, all of the previous virtues listed above.

Shouldn't we all be concerned about the health and welfare of our descendents? That's what life is all about. We must leave our world in a better condition than we found it. Are we doing that today?

We have never heard the leaders of our country blasting, each other with derogatorily words on National TV! Never did we ever hear a president lambaste…HIS OWN party member…because he was religious!

Where in the world is somebody, or anybody? Who will question this kind of behavior by our leaders? Evidently, both sides are guilty of being cowardly?

We all are aware of this condition. Unfortunately, the latest 'poll' show that approval of the president's job, *by his own party members is 90%!!! Other 'POLLS' show over half of the people of our country disapprove of how the president is doing his job. Where is our bipartisanship? Should the entire swamp start 'testing' this political virus? Bipartisan!*

It appears that the sporting world should also be signing up for testing' treatments' now, rather than later.

Switching gears. With the wars during my time (FYI) I served during the Korean War. I spent my two years in Germany securing the borders. (1951-1953). That imaginary border 'WALL' was called a 'Dead Zone.' Which was two hundred yards wide…made of grass only! No trees or bushes!

We had the Russians/ Yugoslavians in our cross hairs, and they had theirs on us…24/7. Should the enemy attack, our job was to delay them until our support was 'scrambled.' We were similar to the canary in the coal mines.

Our training consisted of: Playing war 'games' against the enemy, vie maneuvers. At our stationary base, we were alerted by sirens blaring. We scrambled with tanks, trucks, guns, ammo, food etc…When we reached the 'Dead Zone' we'd come to a screeching halt, and looped back to our base.

Being honest here, I feel guilty to be classified as a veteran, my stint in the service was almost like a vacation, compared to the guys that risked their lives, limbs, and mentality. I personally was affected by four wars; The two World Wars, the Korean, and Vietnam wars. In addition, The Gulf Wars and also the 9-11, disaster.

All 321 million of us in the USA should be ashamed of our selves for not taking care of those hero's, who saved our assess. They gave all of us whatever we have today. Some of us have million dollar homes, the best cars produced, the best yachts ever made, and zillions of dollars in the bank. BUT! **"What are we doing for them"?**

This is so damn sad! We have VA hospitals over flowing with vets that don't know who they are, some limbless, some lifeless etc… and what is sadder, proper and immediate treatments are called out as pathetic.

These hero's deserve the best of everything, including a place to live, other than under a viaduct of the expressways. As we speak, there are negotiations in the works about communities that will be filled with "Tiny Houses." For VETS only. They consist of the necessities only. At least that's a step in the right direction. Let's continue taking care of all of the vets. Let's do something about it!

I don't know if there are any stats about the following or not, but this is my assessment.

It was reported that there are still 400,000 WW ll Vets still alive. They all have to be in their nineties. Within the next ten years, all of those vets will have perished.

Reminiscing here: During WW ll, each household that produced a veteran, displayed a 'banner' about 8"X10" in their front window. The banner was white with a blue star on it. Signifying that there was a vet from this family. If he got killed, the blue star was changed to a gold one. We had a house in the neighborhood that had three gold stars on it. There were many gold stars in our neighborhood. Our front window displayed a banner with two blue stars on it. It represented my two older brothers. We still have it. With the two stars on it. They came back safe and sound. Let's stop and ponder this. No complaints here! Just pondering? Those small 8"X 10" banners in our windows were the 'only' recognition aimed at our hero's for the *FOUR YEARS* of that war! Compare that to today's 'recognition' of today's heroes fighting the COVID-19 war. Today's heroes should, and is being commended to the highest regards for what they are doing, and rightfully so.

Today, just about every governor of the country is on national TV thanking all of us, for doing what he wants us to do, to get through this. And above all, they are also praising to the highest heaven, all of the first responders, the doctors, the nurses, the care takers, and many more of us who are doing things to get us through this crisis. Buildings are lit up in green for compassion, suffering, and the sacrifice of loosing family and friends.

Many stories of good things that happen, like those who beat the virus, are cheered as they leave the hospital, with all of our heroes cheering and clapping for their recovery. The flood gates opened with many tears of happiness. What a wonderful feeling! We *WILL* get through this *TOGETHER!*

History dictates that in the time of crisis, our leaders must be in charge, whether it be a war with troops on the ground, or a virus. If it's 'boots on the ground,' our three and four star generals must make the decisions. They are trained for such operations.

Again, together, we must let those who are scientifically trained in the field of medicine, healthcare, and virus control, to make the decision when it will be safe to return the country, and the world back to normalcy. What ever 'normalcy' will be when this is over?

Being brutally honest, and frank,

WE CANNOT LET ANY POLITICAL LEADER MAKE DECISIONS REGARDING CRISIS OF THIS MAGNITUDE! VIRUS, OR BOOTS.

Getting back to our little 8x10 banner in our windows, recognizing our heroes, what a difference in today's recognition? However, we are still very proud of our little banner.

I would imagine, that most Americans either remember, or saw the picture on the Life magazine front page of the sailor kissing that girl, celebrating the end of WW ll. What will you Millennials do to celebrate your victory over COVID-19 WAR?

Based on the stats, of WW ll vets still alive. The Gulf and Mid-East Wars, are the very last ones, we pray.

Attention millennials: Those Mid-East vets will still be around for another eighty years or more? That's the year 2060? (assuming they are in their twenties when serving.) Don't let them be treated as our vets are being treated today.

The above stats are based on no more wars? Let's all pray for that. However, even the gen X's, know it wont be a war with 'boots on the ground.'

Do you feel like we're a hamster in a cage? Let me get my crystal ball out.

Based on my 'Street Senses' a nuclear war would send the world into oblivion. Let's go virtual here: If it wouldn't be a nuclear war, it will be "STARS WARS!"

The "Stars Wars" would be agreed on (not by a line in the sand!) by the top powers with the most sophisticated space ships. (Prophesying here) Based on today's challengers it would be about five contenders. That is, The United States, Russia, China, North Korea, and Iran. The winner takes all!

They would duke it out in outer space, and the winner would rule the world, and have the right to send the surviving space ships of the enemies, to the sun rays for melt down. Is that cool or what?

Guess what? There would be NO HUMAN DEATHS! I wish I'd be around for that!

On a serious note, there might be another WORLD WAR "0"! IF! The climate change is not addressed with sincerity!

We can't let it be handled like the COVID-19 was at this time. Evidently, the generation before mine, must've dropped the ball very badly, on the Spanish flu in 1918! In the very midst of WW 1. Can you even fathom that?

Even this administration better realize that this pandemic (The Spanish flu), had ***FOUR WAVES of it , over a two year period! With 690, 000 American deaths, and 50 million world wide!***

Those knuckleheads in the swamp, and on the beaches, must take heed to the professionals in the science, and the disease arena. With today's world population, the effects of COVID-19 could make the above figures paltry.

With Covid-19 taking over the attention of all of America, and the world, the border wall is still laying under the carpet.
Since the world is changing so dramatically from day to day, from the scientific-method, culturally, economically, *and political*, wouldn't a border wall be out-dated before the cornerstone was ready for installation?
The 'swamper's' should put that money
 Into the COVID-19 kitty.

Chapter 2

(Our Culture)

Our culture, our gen, was spread evenly across the entire nation. My family was the 'poster' family, or, it was the average American family at that time. Records show that the nation was 95% blue collar workers.

Our city; Louisville, Kentucky was the home plant of the Standard Sanitary (Today it's known as American Standard).
I would estimate that 30-40% of our city's population of males, worked there.

Our city was also the home plant of the L & N Railroad. Known as the (L&N Shops) It was the maintenance hub for all of their engines, service and repairs. Their work force was about the same as Standard's. About 30-40%.

Both of those places of work environment would put the fires of hell, feel like a camp fire for the Boy Scouts.

My dad would come home from work at the Standard, outside temperature was 99 degrees! He would say "It sure is cool outside."

As soon as he came in the house, he'd sit down in his rocking chair, with his clothes still wet from sweat, he'd say who wants to get the brass out today?

One of us kids would get a needle and would prick every splinter of brass out of his arms and legs! He was a brass grinder! That was our DAILY routine. OSHA wasn't even in the incubator. He wore a rubber apron for protection.

Brown and Williams Tobacco, and Phillip Morris were major employers, as was Coca Cola, and three major breweries.
Blue collars were the overwhelming majority of workers.

My children and their friends always ask me this question: "How can you be a part of the greatest generation ever, when you lived during all of the horrific conditions of; World War's l and ll, the Korean War. The Vietnam War. (The later lasting for seventeen years.) The Great Depression. Segregation. The civil rights movements?

We all might want to stop and ponder those questions.

Aside from all of our horrific conditions, I keep telling my children that we had the best living environment ever known to mankind. And, it is really unfortunate, that my generation will be the last generation *EVER* to claim that trophy. You really had to be there! Words for those living conditions are indescribable! Let's walk back to those days. See if you can see our world, through our lenses. Let's go!

Locksmiths were sitting out in front of their store fronts in a rocking chair, smoking cigarettes, a cigar, or a pipe, watching the world go by. NOBODY locked anything! Keys and locks were rusty, from non-use.

Whether your car was in the garage or out on the street, the keys would be in the ignition. You had to leave your house unlocked for the ice man to enter at three and four o'clock in the morning. He'd place the chunk of ice into your ice box. We had a cardboard sign, stuck in the window for the ice man to see. It had four numbers on it: 10, 20, 30, or 40 cents. The 10 cent chunk was where the 12 would be on a clock. It would tell him what size chunk of ice you needed.

The overwhelming majority of the homes never had a refrigerator. That included us.

We had an ice box. Yes it was a wooden box that held a block of ice. It looked like a bedroom dresser. It had a section for a big chunk of ice to sit.

It didn't have drawers, it had three doors. The 'freezer' section was on the inside of where the left door is. That chunk of ice couldn't 'freeze' an ice cycle. It melted when the afternoon heat came along.

There was a drip line under the chunk of ice. When it melted, it dripped into a drip pan underneath the ice box. Each day, one of us kids would have the responsibility of emptying the drip pan into the kitchen sink, before it over flowed. If it ever over flowed, you faced a consequence.

It is the break of dawn. You can smell the smoke coming out of chimneys of just about every home, circa the 1930's. You could see soot on rooftops and cars. Ninety-nine percent of homes had fireplaces or coal stoves. We had only a small coal stove for the entire house.

There were four houses in our entire neighborhood that still had outside crappers. Ours was one. You haven't lived if you have never tried pooping in a shanty with cracks between the boards about an inch wide, and the wind and snow snapping at your bare butt…when you took your first steps in this world. "Personal hygiene" consisted of using pages from the old Sears Catalogs, or pages from the newspaper. We couldn't afford any brand of toilet paper. Not even the cheapest brand at the brick and mortar box stores. OOPS! There were no brick and mortar boxed stores yet!I don't want to get too graphic here, but I feel compelled to, for you to understand why we were the G GEN!

The outhouse, or shanty, was normally about six feet square, and maybe seven feet high, made out of 1"X6" pine boards.

Most were 'two' seaters, and made out of the same type wood. It looked like you were sitting on a closed wooden casket, with two holes cut out of the top of it.

The outhouse did have a wooden floor, same type as all of the other boards. A hole was dug about six feet deep, and about five feet square. Two 2'X4's" about eight feet long would be nailed to the shanty, (temporarily) and used as handles. It took four people to carry the shanty, to place it over that pit, then you'd remove those handles. It was not anchored.

Here's the gruesome part of it all. When the pit was about three feet deep with excrement, a man wearing waders, we called them hip boots. Most likely it was a black man. Discrimination was still in vogue. He would get down in there, standing in the excrement, with a water bucket on a rope. He'd scoop the poop up in the bucket and holler, "Pull her up!" Another guy was holding the other end of the rope. And yes, the whole crew were black men. He'd pull it up, and pour it into a wheel barrel, and it would be wheeled out to a truck in the alley. I am trying to be explicit here for you to have a keen picture of how my generation was just a few short years ago. And for you to envision what your generation will look like a few years from now? This is another feather in our cap, to prove why we were the G.G!

Our generation's lifestyle made us stronger individuals both mentally and physically…but more importantly…it built character. Roll back to our earlier lifestyle.

Unfortunately, that black soot from the coal stoves and fireplaces, also landed on the most immaculate landscaping you could ever imagine. Ninety-nine percent of the homes and landscaping, would qualify for the front page on the home and gardening magazine.

In addition to the lawn looking like the #12 hole at Augusta National, every other home had a garden of vegetables, fruit, or flowers. If any of us kids even looked sideways at the fruit trees, or flowers, it was a misdemeanor. If we hit a baseball, or if we missed a shot at the basketball goal in the alley, (a bushel basket with the bottom removed),and it entered those hollowed grounds, it would take an act of congress to get the home owner to retrieve our ball for us. If it happened the second time, 'the warden' (homeowner) would confiscate it until your dad got home from work. When that happened, the crime automatically was upped to a felony.

When we saw our dad coming home from work, we immediately headed for the coal shed. His choice of 'correctional tools' were hanging on the inside wall of the shed: A Louisville Slugger, a table tennis paddle, or a jockey's whip. Your sentence was based on how much he had to drink before coming home from work. Most of the father's in the neighborhood worked in hell's fire foundries.

Henceforth, a visit to the corner saloon on the way home from work was inevitable.

Let me set the stage here for other 'crime scene (s).' Based on the severity of the crime.

Because we were as poor as a church mouse, fresh fruits were scarce. At nighttime, my younger brother Jerry and I and a very close friend, would steal fruits whenever we could, from the neighbor's yards. There was an array to select from: Some homes had Apples, some Peaches, Persimmons, Grapes, etc… But! None of the above!

Two houses down from our house, the owner of the property looked like 'Popeye the Sailor Man.' And he was a zillion times meaner and tougher than Popeye. (He didn't need spinach or anything else). And we knew that going in. That's how desperate we were for fruits. He had the most scrumptious cherries ever known to mankind. Three trees of them! He had a vertical six foot wooden fence around his entire backyard. Not picket fences, but solid 1"X8" vertical slats…side-by-side. The wooden doorway was made with the same boarding, but he had that door locked from the inside of the fence. It wasn't really a lock, it was a latch. To go out of that door., you just had to flip a latch up. So, we had to scale that fence to get into paradise. We intruded his property many times unbeknownst to him.

HOWEVER! This time my brother and I (and best friend), were wearing a 'beanie cap.' (Goober Pyle) wore in Mayberry R.F.D. They were cool at that time. We were wearing a replica of it. Ours had the year 1941 stitched on the front of it? We still don't know where mom bought them and why that year on them? Maybe for Pearl Harbor? The Japanese War?

As we were filling our beanie caps with cherries, Popeye comes out of his house with his garbage, to take back to the alley. He came after us. He had the jump on us, so we didn't have time to get to that door that was latched.

We raced for that fence as fast as we could and scaled over it like a commando would. Brother Jerry landed sideways in the alley and twisted his ankle! But, we managed to get far enough down the alley that he didn't come after us. However! During our escape mode, Brother Jerry lost his beanie cap under one of Popeye's trees! (with cherries in it). EVERYBODY in the neighborhood knew that we were the only ones who had those caps. Yes, including Popeye! By this time, brother Jerry and I could envision our dad's choice of correctional tools, the dreaded Louisville Slugger!

No offense to dad, and to ALL of the men in the hood, but they all were worried about ever facing Popeye! Just to mention his name, in any manner, you could see a yellow streak growing up their backs.

There was a store up around the corner from our street, named Mac Kendrick's. It was an ice cream and candy store. We called it "The Sweet Shop." It was our "Safe-Place" to meet when in trouble. In fact all of the kids in the hood would hang around the sweet shop every evening and sometimes during the day.

(*Snitz' Basketball team @ "Safe Place."*)

The sweet shop had three small wrought iron tables with matching chairs, plus two pinball machines, we hunkered down on those chairs.

As brother Jerry and I awaited for the other shoe to fall, our bowels started churning. Soon, what appeared to be what looked like a gorilla, was in the doorway. Our blood was no longer effective, we were drained. We heard a very

strong and bull horned like sound: "RAMON! JERRY! Get out here! NOW!
(Whenever dad used our full given name, our stomachs would start churning!)

In the silence of the night, walking on the sidewalk, I walked on Dad's left,
Jerry on his right side. Not one word was spoken…dead silence!

When we reached the house before our house, dad performed a "Mark Spitz"
back stroke, and slapped both if us simultaneously on the back of our heads.

I went sprawling to the gutter of the street, and Jerry ended up on a grassy
knoll of the neighbors front yard. Both of us thought we heard the clanging
of the bell on the electric street car up the street!

When we got inside our house, Dad must have thought it was the fifteenth
round? He 'slapped us silly' with his bare hand! Over every inch of our body,
except our face. He had never ever hit us with his fist, anywhere, or slapped us
in the face. He was over six feet tall, and weighed 250 pounds.

Lo and behold, our 'best' friend was looking through our window, and laughing
hysterically at the beating we were getting. He followed us home with dad,
from the 'Safe Place.'

Course, the reason dad found out what we did, which we knew, previously, Popeye
brought dad the indisputable evidence that we were the perps. …Jerry's cap.

After this episode, brother Jerry and I learned an invaluable lesson about
discipline. We never stole another piece of fruit, yes, not even one cherry, nor
ANYTHING else the rest of our entire lives. Believe me, stronger disciplinary
measures must be reactivated in today's world. Today's 'Soft' disciplinary
measures are useless. Proof is in the pudding.

The daily routine for families were; only men would be leaving the house for
work. Most women were stay-at-home moms. They would be getting the kids
ready for school. This was pre Pearl Harbor.

Since that "Day of Infamy," December 7, 1941, women were off to war with
the men draftees. Some were WAVES; (women accepted volunteers emergency
services), WAACS; (women army auxiliary corps). WASP; (women army

service pilots). The women were not sent into combat. They were always in an auxiliary position. The women army pilots, were used as test pilots only.

The women were NOT drafted, they volunteered. The women who stayed behind, worked in manufacturing plants, building defense materials, such as trucks, jeeps, airplanes, firearms, gun powder etc.…

The ladies who worked in those plants, doing a man's job, were called "Rosie the Riveters!" Their 'motto' or chant was: "WE CAN DO IT!" Everyone was patriotic. And, ALL IN!

Are all of you ladies putting yourself in those ladies shoes? Would you choose those careers? What would you do?

POP-UP! Did you know that there is no such an item as a 1942, 1943, 1944, 1945 automobile! Nor a truck for those same years! Raise your hand if you knew that answer. Contrarily, those early years of WW ll brought the entire United States of America together as one big family. Patriotism, and respect for each and everyone of us, flourished beyond recall!

There was a rationing of gasoline. They gave you a sticker for your windshield, and a small coupon book for how many gallons of gas that you could get. As follows: the letter "A" was for pleasure only. You were allowed only four gallons a week. That coupon book had ration stamps in it. You had ration stamps for just four gallons only. (How many gallons do you use a week?) The letter "B" was for anyone who worked for the government in any capacity. They were entitled to eight gallons a week. The letter "C" was for physicians, ministry, public workers etc. They were allowed eight gallons a week also. So if you ran out of gas pleasure driving, before the week was up, you had to park it the rest of that week. Can you guys even fathom that condition?

There was a theater down town that showed nothing but news about the war. News reporters, and cameramen were embedded with the troops. No TV yet! The theater's name: "The Scoop."

"Strategically." On the left side of the "Scoop" theater, was a recruiting station for the Army and Navy. On the right side of the movie house was a recruiting station for the Marines. When you came out of the movie house, after watching all of the fighting and carnage of our troupes going on around the world, lines would form at both recruiting stations! EVERYBODY was 'all in!'

Talking with many-many WW ll veterans, they will tell you that they lied about their age, just so they could enlist in all branches of service! Many as young as fifteen years old! Today, those survivor's tell us: "It was not a sacrifice! But our duty!"

And! ***EVERYBODY ANSWERED THE CALL!*** Draft age went from 21, to as high as the early thirties, and downward to 18. The toll of injuries, and deaths of the soldiers, were causing chaos in the assignments of troops.

The reason for the age group to be drafted was so volatile, was the progress of the battles of war. Our armed forces were spread thinly around the globe.

Just in case you forgot, or didn't read the history books, The United States armed services were assisting our allies in Europe before December 7, 1941.

Unfortunately, our allies had their hands full with battles all over Europe!

Contrarily, assisting us in our fight in the Pacific War with Japan, was minuscule.

Hitler was on the verge of accomplishing his mission: "Today Europe! Tomorrow the World!" Unless you lived then, you can't phantom how near the brink was. It appeared he would do it! Some of us started learning the German language!

Pre 1941. Keep in mind here: There were no TV, smart phones, tablets, I-pods Etc….for future reference, let's call the *(Electronic gadgets)* "E-GADS." Socially, we had only two "E-Gads"! Think about this! We had just two of them! A land radio, and a land phone! Both had to be plugged into a wall plug. *(NEITHER WOULD FIT INTO OUR POCKET OR PURSE!).* Our 'social media' was the local newspaper…and radio ONLY! Normally, the newspaper was delivered twice a day; morning, and evening. If there was a crises in the world, such as December 7, 1941, the newspaper delivery boys would be called in to deliver a special edition of the newspaper: Aptly named: "EXTRA!"

They walked down the middle of the streets (hardly any cars were on the streets) hollering: "EXTRA ! EXTRA! Read all about it!" (It would cost you a nickel or a dime?) The 'extra' was about that crisis only!

For all of you millennials, and even the baby boomers, Let that sink in! No, face book, no instagrams, no tweeters, twatters, I-pads, I-phones! Can you even fathom that?

Only a few homes had a land phone. If you did, you had to share your line with three other homes! If you picked up your phone, you could ease drop on their conversations!

The land phones would ring according to your assigned 'number' of party lines: Party line #1, you'd answer when it rang only one time. Party line #2, two rings, etc… AND! a real person! Usually, a lady would ask you: "Number Please!" She'd dial it for you! *Take that you robo #$@$$##!*

(Compare those conversations to today's world of 'images' sent out on the I-phones!) No explanation needed here. You young'ns know what I am talking about. Namely you gen X's! The millennials were native E-Gadgets.

Let's all stop here in our tracks, and think about this evolution. Just think about the magnitude of changes taking place here day in and out! It's mind boggling! Maybe we can wrap our brain around some of the credits for the E-gads. There are overwhelming pluses! And subtleminuses. The later? A downward spike in exercising our brain, and our bodies. And, that loss of personal contact.

Many E-Gads are very good, and very helpful and rewarding. However, just like any 'investment,' there is a downside. The experts always bring up *"VALUE"* when investing. And then add, beside financially, there is an 'emotional factor.'

Again, speaking for my generation, we believe that the *"WORST"* 'APP' is the 'Tweeting.' (I'm hunkered down, trying to dodge all of those 'missiles' that are heading my way, I'll be back shortly)?

However! That 'personal' (emotion) factor is not in the equation! I don't want to be a Debby Downer here, and I haven't heard ANYONE say this YET! And I hope it will never happen to any of us. But I'm sure it will happen:

Unless you've been living under a rock for the last few years, we all have witnessed school shootings, some on TV, and others in person. The frantic parents, running to the school, not knowing if their child was lying dead, or alive?

*Let's ALL hug and kiss our kids, and all other family members,
and our close friends, goodbye no matter when they leave us whether
to bed, school, work, or get in a car.*

Since Covid-19 has been added to the mix, and we are 'socially distancing,' the above narrative must return to all of us after the virus is conquered.

To my knowledge, there was NEVER EVER a mass school shooting back in our days. In fact, I don't know of any mass shootings back in our day! Except Valentines Day. But, that was gang related. Gangster Al *(Scarface)* Capone was responsible for a massacre on St. Valentines Day, where seven were murdered, which was gang related.

Back to the E-Gads. I got hit by a few tomatoes and eggs…but, I'm good.

Reiterating here: The very first scientific *'invasion'* of our (GG) planet was by a guy named "Buck Rogers." He was preceded by "Star Wars!" "Buck" started out in comic books in 1928, and then into the movies.

"Buck" predicted what will happen in the 25th century! Just think about that. He is living in the 20th century! He's predicting what will happen 500 years in the future! HUM! That's not too far off! Let's put this in perspective. Let's compare my living conditions, to yours.

We had; 'Morris Code,' a ticker-tape message system. The light bulb was invented. YES! Pre the invention, we watched the old lamp lighter do his job! Every evening at dusk, he'd have to lower the street lamp, by a rope, and install a gas-light type fuse. At the break of dawn, do that same maneuver, and put-out the light of that fuse. That was an *event* for us! Are you having fun yet? We were. After he installed a new fuse, normally he would put the burnt-out fuse into a large canvas bag, and take them back to the shop to be destroyed. However, sometimes he would give us the old burnt out fuse. There might have been a little 'powder' left in the fuse. We'd light it up with a match and it looked like a fire cracker burning, no chance of exploding. NOW! We are really having fun!

Course, it wasn't long when they replaced it with a light bulb. They switch on and off by themselves! No more fun for us!

Aside here. During the war years, 1941-1945, we would have 'Air Raid' drills.

Hitler's airplanes were alleged planning to attach strategic locations in the United States. Namely the ammunition plant across the river from us, in Indiana.

A number of people on your street served as "Air Raid" wardens. When the air raid sirens went off, they would wear an identifiable colored jacket. It was their duty to make sure every light inside your house was off, and all of your blinds and shades were closed. If they weren't, he'd bang on your door and holler to turn them off, and shutter.

Back to our other E-Gadgets. For the first few years that we had Televisions, 1948, you had to keep moving the rabbit ears around, based on the weather report. Naturally, someone would have to get out of the chair to change the direction of the rabbit ears. You'd also have to get up and change the station by a knob ON the TV. No remotes. Let's engage our imagination here. I'm standing in the back of the TV, and you are sitting on the couch, telling me how to slowly and cautiously move one ear, and then the other, to get the best picture:

> *"NO, back a little more, NO! a little more to the right! Not that much! Dad! make him move it slower! He's trying to piss all of us off!"* (We really didn't use that word in the present of our mom and dad!)

Most of the first TV screens were seven-to-ten inches. They were called;

> *"Tabletop" TV's. No floor models yet.* (Are you kidding? You
> have an *"86 inch TV"*! *Hang it on the wall! Are you kidding me!*
> *NO WAY! A remote control also? Ain't NO way!"*).

For our 'table top TV,' you could buy a magnifying glass that had two 'sled-runners' or shoes on the bottom of it, that you could slide it under the small screen! Suddenly, you had a fifteen inch screen! Although, distorted. The picture looked like one of those mirrors in an amusement park. But a distorted picture was better than no picture at all.

Need we mention, what devices you have on your person? In your pocket, purse, around your neck? In your ear? NOW! Did you know, as we speak, they just had a conversation with the astronauts in outer space…via YOUR smart phone? That was the first time ever!

Are we moving too quickly? Are the E-Gads too far advanced for us to keep up with? Are we prepared for them; *personnel-wise?* Can you believe that I am still here to tell you all about those 'old days'…compared to yours! So! What will it be like in just a short fifty years? We must always think about the future. Can you believe that I was here when we had to crank a car or truck, to start the engine? AND!

ALL AIRPLANES STILL HAD PROPELLERS !

If you millennials continue with all of these newer E-gads; robots, driverless cars and airplanes, and most of all, biological! Artificial hearts? Legs, Arms? I might be here to see if "Buck Rogers" was right! G-O-L-LY! I can't wait, hurry up!

I mentioned earlier about me being ninety-one years old. People always ask me: "What kind of life did you live, to live so long?" My response is always truthful, because I really do hate liars. You cannot ever believe a liar. What good is he or she?

True Story: Here's my recipe for longevity. You must exercise at least three times a week, for forty-five minutes. I've been doing this for the last 22 years. I would have NEVER exercised, if it wasn't for a torn cartilage in my knee. My doctor told me that he'd give me cortisone shots in my knee, and send me to a physical therapist. If that doesn't fix the problem, an operation will be necessary.

An operation was never needed. I was sixty-seven years old. I never entertained any kind of diet. I do believe you have to have a good sense of humor, and *LOVE* music, for longevity. Beside of what I ate, and my sense of humor, and music, here is my daily routine. *Mix this up and shake it!* Many years ago I met a guy from Lynchburg TN. He must've been a racecar driver? They called him 'J.D,' and he wore a black shirt with the #7 on it. He had a couple of friends from St. Louis, MO. He called both of them "Bud"? Their last names were; Lite and Wiser. We all get together at my house EVERY DAY! For cocktail hour(s). Based on my mood at that time, the 'drink' of the day would be decided. I would choose either "Two fingers of 'JD' on the rocks with a splash of water."

OR! If I was *extremely* happy, or sad? It would be a straight 'shooter' of 'JD,' and one of his "Buds" chasing him down the hatch. Those guys *"MAKE MY DAY!"* We crank up the Bose radio to it's highest level, and open all doors and windows during the summer months. Sometimes one of us would get up and try to dance…to the 60's & 70's music.

You must select the music that takes you back to the decade(s) of your life when you were at the peak of happiness in your own life. It's amazing how soothing and satisfying this type of party will change your attitude, lift you up and out of the stresses of living in this present world.

All of us, boys and girls, thought that the singers, when singing romantic songs, were singing to us…personally! They had exciting eyes, and inviting smiles. If we weren't in love with them, or nobody at that time, we were just 'in love with love.' The whole world was romantic. Today's generation must bring those days back of loving and tenderness. That 'sensitive' neuron. HOWEVER! All of this (drinking) must be done in moderation…or I wouldn't be here at my typewriter.

My 'characters' and I have been meeting like this since my wife passed away eight years ago. I couldn't have handle these eight years without them, after being with her for 61 of the best years of our lives…*True Story!*

Last year, my daughter hosted my ninetieth birthday party at her house. Many of the invited guest asked me what my birthday wish would be?

My response is always: "I want to live only nine more years, and be a hundred years old. Then get my head blown off by a jealous lover."

Let's pull back to the pre-war years. (*Oh! I forgot! As I stated earlier about liars, is true! And everything about my way of life is also true! I wouldn't be 'typing' this if it wasn't true*). Some men car-pooled to work, or rode an electric over-head street car. Mom's kept the house. When the kids came home from school, mom's had a snack for them before they raced outside to play with their friends. (*Our family was not included in this type of a 'daily routine.' Explanation later*). Mom's had 'supper' ready for the kids and dad, when he walked in the door. (*Dad would really be mad, if his food wasn't on table, when he walked in that door!*)

After supper, the entire family would clean up the mess. Not dad! He was 'King.' Let's pause here; if you are still wondering why we were the greatest generation, it started right here: *"SUPPERTIME!"*

We called it suppertime, many people might call it 'dinner.' In any case, it was the last meal on weekdays. On Sunday, the noontime meal was: *"DINNERTIME"*

No matter who called it what, or whatever? That's not the point here.

This meal was our generation's version of a "Pottery Kiln." These were the times when the entire family was gathered together, it was our daily routine. We were molded into who we are today.

Close your eyes. Are you ready? I can see you peeking! Vision this:

> *There was no distraction of any kind at table. All you could hear was the chatter between all the family members. Discussing school, work, or social activities. Wisdom was ambient, pouring over all of us. There was laughter, and comforting. Mom and dad learned something about us, and we really learned much more from them. That was the mantra back then. Learning right from wrong… right here at table!*
> *Personally, I believe that we, my three brothers and I, gained the virtues of honesty and discipline at this time.*
>
> *Lo and behold, if we didn't gain wisdom during these times…we would've been left to wonder aimlessly…out into the wilderness… alone! Could that be you?*

Whether you be a millennial or not, you must put the family back in your life at HOME. This is where you are molded into who you will really in your lifetime. What is the overwhelming majority of all of our problems in today's world? Mostly drugs, that lead to myriads of crimes. It's at this time, 'at table' when the seed is sowed. We cultivate it from the table. We can't expect the schools, society, the community, to take care of us. I don't want to sound derogatory, but we didn't have the myriads of 'life savors' back in our days. We stood in soup lines that wrapped around the entire city. And, all we got was just that: SOUP! No sides, or trimmings!

Back to the best days ever. After 'suppertime' moms and dads would proceed to the swings out on the front porch. We never had a swing nor a front porch! Mom and dad were OK with that.

However, *There was an inherent invitation to ALL neighbors to come join in!* You were always welcome to sit on a chair on their porch or out in their grass, which was commonplace. And, no distancing! Our family never had a swing, or a front porch. Mom and dad would sit in our side yard, on our wooden kitchen chairs. They couldn't afford lawn chairs. If we kids wasn't playing out in the street with the other kids, we'd sit with mom and dad in the side yard. We never sat in the front yard. Mom was ashamed because of dad's drinking problem. All of the adults would sit and talk and watch the kids play in the middle of the street. Traffic was miniscule. For the few families who had cars, they were parked for the night, in the garage or a few would be parked out on the street.

Most jobs were very laborious. For parents, going out for entertainment was rare during weekdays. The street was full of kids, it looked like a school yard! Back then, *MOST* families were *VERY LARGE!* Besides playing some kind of game with a ball out in the street, or play, 'ring around the rosy,' 'drop the handkerchief' 'hide and seek,' we also played a game called "Dainty." It was a game brought over from Germany by our forefathers. Our neighborhood (Snitzelburg) was 99% Germans. Your 'equipment' consisted of an old mop or broom handle only. You'd cut a six inch piece off of the handle. That was called the "Dainty." Then you'd whittle both ends of it to a point.

Taking what's left of the broom handle, no straw, just the handle of it, you'd whittle one end of it to a point. Hold the opposite end for a bat. Lay the "Dainty" on a spot in the middle of the street, and designate that as; 'Home

Plate.' With the "Dainty" lying on home plate, pointing to center field, take the 'bat,' the broom stick, striking downward, leading with the pointed end, to the "Dainty's" pointed end. When it flips up in the air, quickly hit the "Dainty" in mid-air as far as you can! Let's say you hit it twenty-five yards! The following 'batter' must hit it farther than you did. If not? He must hop… on one foot… out to where you hit the "Dainty." Having fun yet? We were! It didn't take much for us to have fun! The life style was very simple, and relaxing for all.

The mom's and dad's, on their front porch swings, would chat with all of the neighbors within earshot, including across the street about trivial stuff. The streets were not very wide…they were built for horse and buggies.

Everybody was just being neighborly. The homes were so close to each other, you could hear your neighbor pass gas.

Neighborhood's were like the rest of the United States, a real family.

Sometime later, the mom's would walk down to the corner grocery for food for the next day. They engaged with other neighbors along the way; *gossiping!*

Most homes had wooden ice boxes to keep their food cold. They'd buy non-frig items before turning in for the night. Just about all of the grocer's would deliver your groceries for 5-10 cents, by one of the kids in the hood, who had a bike. But! If you had it delivered, the women would miss out on all of the latest gossip along the way. That was their entertainment. In the wee hours of the morning, the ice man would place a chunk of ice in your ice box, while everybody was asleep. We didn't have to lock our doors and windows… cars, or the garage, ever!

Many never had enough food for the entire family, due to the great depression. There were 'soup lines' serpentine through-out neighborhoods all over the country. Our ice box was bare most of the time. When it was bare, the ice melted, we'd take the shelves out and play in it! We'd take turns of locking each other in it…you couldn't unlock it from the inside! So, when you were ready to get out, about the time that you couldn't breathe any more, you'd holler out: "Open the door!" Brother Don, a prankster, wouldn't open it until you almost passed out!

When we talk about those times today, we wonder why mom or dad never screamed at us for doing that! We could have suffocated in there!

FYI; about the 'ice box.' There was a section in it where the iceman would sit the chunk of ice. Naturally there was no electricity to the box. So, the chunk of ice would melt over a period of time, right.

There was a drain tube to a wash pan under the ice box. Ever so often, you'd flip a little flap door up, that was attached to the front bottom of the ice box, to see if the pan needs to be empty. There was no way to know how long it would take to fill up? So, we'd check it many times during the day. That was the duty of one of us kids. If you ever let that pan overflow to the floor, you'd start walking to the coal shed. You knew, you were going to get punished.

The door on the right was our 'jail cell.' Brother Don wouldn't open it until we almost passed out.

While we're on this subject, here's a little 'food' for thought.

My family was hungry all of the time. Most of us scraped and licked our plates as clean as a hound's tooth, because we were so hungry Not a crumb was left! To this day, we still do the same, even when we go out for dinner. I lied. We don't lick the plate anymore, when we go out. Anyway, back to my lie. I'm not lying about this. I'm betting the farm that all of my generation feels this way:

When we open the frig today, and see every shelf jammed with food, we say a prayer for all of our blessings. To this day, we can still remember opening that old ice box…*It was completely empty!* Those pictures are indelible to this day.

Thankful, not only for the abundance of food today, but also the spout for cold water, and the ice maker…crushed or cubes! And, no worry about the drip-pan!

Previously, we had to use an ice pick and chip off ice, put it in a glass, and go to the sink for cold water or drinks. On the plus side, we don't need an ice man anymore.

Back then, when the alarm went off for dad and the kids to get up for school and work, mom would hurry down to the grocery store and get the meats and dairy products, so she could fix each one breakfast. YES! In rain, snow, sunshine or sleet! This was a daily routine for her.

(Just think a little longer about that!)

Earlier we talked about the rationing of gasoline? Well it was also a rationing of certain foods! Such as; meats, sugars, or many other articles associated with food.

In addition to rationings, there was also a shortage of iron and steel products to build tanks, guns, trucks, etc.. If you had a wrought iron fence, the government would asked you to sell it. If you refused, they'd take it anyway. Things were very tight at these times.

During the winter months, before she could fix our breakfasts, she had to build a fire in the pot belly coal stove. That was her job. It was us kids job, to make sure that mom had the coal and wood in the house, before bedtime.

(Is your imagination engaged?)

The men were responsible for providing food on the table, and the rent, or a mortgage payment. Since our dad was an alcoholic, he couldn't keep up his end of the above commitment for rent.

We all lived with our parents for our first twenty-one years of our lives, that's when we all got married. Dad NEVER EVER brought his full gross paycheck home. Just the net check. Mom went to her grave, never ever seeing his gross paycheck stub! She never knew that he had an active, an on-going loan at the Credit Union where he worked. Course, that on-going 'loan' was for his drinking, and also his gambling.

Our grocer, would allow him 'credit' for two weeks of food. He got paid every two weeks. That was commonplace for all grocer's customers. If our bill was $10.00 for those two weeks, *(and it probably was back in these days)* it reached a point where we couldn't pay the full amount! Mom would give us whatever she had to give it to the grocer. Soon, we got so far behind that the grocer cut us off!

With a grocery on just about very corner, he went to another grocer, on another corner, a little farther away. The same thing happened here. Soon he had to take bankruptcy. Yes, this was in the 1930's.

Mom was able to get her dad, *our grand paw, remember him?* to help bail him out with payments to the loan sharks, which was over three hundred dollars.

Can you imagine what that $'value' was back then? We were still making payments for him until he died.

Back to times before bankruptcy.

If you would glance back to my "BIO," it stated that my dad swore under oath, that I was sixteen years old? However, I had just turned fifteen, only one month after my 15th birthday. If you're trying to figure that out…I was fifteen, and one month old when I got my drivers licenses. What was your vision for your future when you just turned fifteen years old? Most likely, your prom and graduation day? Our vision was working. We knew we would never reach proms and graduation days. Our maximum formal education was completing our freshman year only.

Back up here to my leaving school. I was fourteen years old when I left high school after the freshmen year, September of 1943. The very next day, I got a job. I had to get a 'working permit' from the local authorities. It was mandatory because you had to be sixteen years old before you could get a real adult job.

I was hired in as a helper on a delivery truck for a commercial laundry and linen service company. Starting pay was $12.00 a week…straight salary! That means my working hours were: "Whatever it takes to get the job done." It took fifty hours or more! My job was to report to the laundry by 6:00 am. Load the truck up with thousands of clean hand towels. The driver would come in, and we were off to Brown and Williams tobacco co. @ 16th and Hill Streets in Louisville KY. I would unload the truck of thousands of clean towels, and I was left there. The driver would leave to service his other laundry accounts in this section of town. The building was in a city-long block, four story brick building. I had to visit EVERY RESTROOM, men's and women on EVERY Floor. Take the dirty towels out of cabinets, and put them in a laundry basket with wheels on it. Then restock the cabinet with clean towels. By the time that I finished servicing the entire four stories of the building, it was time to go back and start all over again! If I had a real good day, without any problems, I was finished by 6:00 pm.

The driver would come back and get me at 6:00 pm., and the thousands of dirty towels, and we'd head back to the *"BARN"* (The laundry plant).

We called it the *"BARN"* back then, because that's when the cows would come home, just before dark, just as we did also.

At these times, Brown and Williamsons was one of the largest employers in the city…four thousand employees! Smoking cigs was filling our lungs with cancer, including me.

Our dad smoked, mom didn't. Before we got a job, we asked him to let us try one. He said no, and added; "When you get a job and can afford them, then you can." Guess what? I HAVE A JOB, AND SMOKING. The price, in 1943, was 10-15 cents for a pack of twenty! (*"HOW IN THIS WORLD CAN YOU GUYS AFFORD TO PAY $5.00, OR MORE FOR A PACK OF CIGS TODAY?"*) If you are still smoking, this might help *YOU* save your life, or money. I smoked for about twenty-five years, from 14 to about 40 years old…before I quit! That was about fifty years ago. YOU! Can quit. Here's what I did, and you can to. Lent is for 40 days of penance, I quit smoking. I quit EVERY Lent…all forty days! Then I'd see how long I could go after Lent! I went as long as a year after lent! Not smoking! And yet, I still started back!

Just TRY it, you might be surprised. Think about this! If you would put an apostrophe in the word impossible, you'd get; I'm possible! How about that? *(Remember! I'm ninety-one years old! In pretty good health. No lung cancer!* CDC claims, if you do quit, you can restore your lungs back to normal! It did for me!

Since our dad was an alcoholic, when we got a job, we had to give mom a portion of our take home pay. For our food etc… Her cut was EIGHTY PERCENT! Ours was the remaining 20%.

SO! MY net take home pay, as a helper, was $12.00 a week, So! For my fifty hours of work, or more, my personal earnings were $2.40! Mom's was $9.60!

In January 1944, a national linen service bought our laundry. They raised my salary as a helper to $19.00 a week, again, straight salary! Again, fifty or more hours a week. Now I'm making big money! 20% of $19.00 is; $3.80! Almost twice as much as I was making! Very soon after that I was promoted to a truck driver! Now my salary is $31.00 a week, again, the same arrangements. 20% of 31.00, is $6.20! For fifty hours or more!

Now, I can really afford those THREE PACKS OF CIGS A DAY! Or more! That was my daily consumption!!! And yes, still fifty hours or more a week.

One time my mom called my boss at 9:00 PM, and wanted to know where I was? Why I wasn't home yet? He told her that I'd be home shortly. I started at 6:00 AM. *(Remember now, I'm just 15 years old)*

Mom was getting 80% of our take home pay because our two oldest brothers were in the army. When they were discharged from the army, and we were all teenagers, or older, mom reversed our slice of the pie, we got the 80%, she got the 20 %! Soon, mom was able to discontinue her portion of our take home pay.

It was when we started dating seriously, and getting ready for marriage.

Let's pull back to when we were growing from the cradle to marriage.

The rent for our house was $12.00 per month! Here's why it was so cheap!

It had two front bedrooms, a 'living room' and a kitchen…It had NO BATHROOM!

We had the 'outhouse' for #2, and a slop jar behind a cabinet inside for #1.

Mom and dad educated us to do #2 before dark, and bedtime. They'd have to go back there with us to use the outhouse! Whoever had to take us to the outhouse, would have to carry matches, newspaper, or an old phone book, and a candle. *(We couldn't afford TP as NEEDED, nor owned a flashlight)*. Trips to the outhouse was; in rain, snow, sunshine or sleet! In inclement weather, words are indescribable for those events. Our butts weren't the only thing that had a crack in it. Rest assured, all of us are still having problems with hemorrhoids to this day.

We did the 'bird bath' at the kitchen sink during the week, NO! Not while we were eating, but on Saturday's, *whether we needed it or not, we were bathed* in a galvanized wash tub sitting on the kitchen floor.

That little potbelly coal stove in the living room (next to the kitchen) was all of the heat we had for the entire house! Mom would light all of the gas burners on the kitchen stove for warmth, while bathing.

In the winter months, mom would close off that very front bedroom from November to March to save the heat for all of the other three rooms in the house. That front bedroom looked just like a walk-in freezer. Two of us slept in there! The two front windows, and the front door, were a solid sheet of ice for those three-to-four months of winter. Frozen shut! You couldn't open them! It was like that until we all got married…20 years! PLUS! Two of us slept in the same bedroom with mom and dad! Our beds were *'footboard-to-footboard'!* Just enough room to walk through, sideways. Attention Millennials! Mom and dad were in their THIRTIES!…Two of us slept in that same bedroom, from the cradle, until we all got married!

Engage your imagination here. Your sleeping arrangements? You, in your thirties, and you have two of your pre-teenage sons sleeping in your same bedroom! *(That could be why our dad was an alcoholic?)* Can you blame him?

Remember. Those sleeping arrangements were like that until we all got married! So, eventually, you had your two grown teenage son's sleeping in your bedroom. I was 22 years old! (That's when I got married). How about those apples?

Switching gears here, if Google would have been around back in our days, it would have shown that on just about every corner was a grocery store, with a butcher shop in it. All meats weren't cut, until you ordered it. Fresh from the hides.

In fact, every vital product to live, and grow healthy, or just survive, was available within a block or two of walking distance. In addition to the grocery store, there was a pharmacy, bakery, candy store, church, and a neighborhood movie house, and most importantly for the men, was a corner saloon. Which was very busy during and after the great depression years. (*And also if your kids are sleeping at the foot of your bed*).

Just about every saloon sold sandwiches, many had roast beef, with gravy! Fried chicken was a specialty! In just about EVERY saloon, a big gallon size jar sat on the bar, that contained "Pickled pig's feet!" And! They were free! Just as those jars of XL figure 8 pretzels were!

The reasoning was to buy more beer and alcohol! Dinning-out was not an option for us. No fast foods, not even a MicD's! During these times, it was normal for our parents to send us kids down to the corner saloon. Some had a two-quart-size light weight galvanized (beer) bucket, or a glass water pitcher, dad had a glass pitcher to buy draft beer to bring home.

We were pre-teen, and early teens! The 'law' was very lax about these episodes.

Our dad was a very close friend of one of the bartenders; "Kirch." Dad would tell us: "If 'Kirch' is on duty, tell him that the beer is for me. He always gives me and extra good measure."

A full pitcher of beer cost a quarter, sometimes dad had only fifteen cents. So he'd get only a half of a pitcher.

So, when he didn't have a quarter, he'd give us fifteen cents and tell us to tell "Kirch" it was for our dad. He would fill'er up for him for only fifteen cents!

On the way back home, carrying the pitcher of beer, my brother and I would stop every now and then and sneak a few swigs out of it! By the time we got home, the pitcher was half empty! We'd tell dad: "'Kirch' was NOT on today!"

Oh yes, the family doctor would come to your house! He'd have a small satchel that would be full of meds that would cure any problem that you had. If you had a serious problem, like I did, scarlet fever, all of us were quarantined for ten days! A red sign was placed on all doors. No one could enter, and we couldn't leave.

Here is just another notch in our "Tool Belt." *Brotherly love.* We were all out playing ball in the street when the doctor came for our monthly check up. Mom called Don in for his. Soon Don comes running out to us playing in the street and hollers: "Hey Ray, I have to have my tonsils taking out, you want to go with me and have yours taken out?" I said sure, "let's go!" We didn't go at that time, but later we both did have our tonsils taken out at the same time, even though I didn't HAVE to have mine taken out.

If someone died, you were laid out in the front room! A white lily wreath was displayed on the front door. *(I don't know what mom and dad would do if someone died during the winter months?)* As we grew out of playing in the street and yards, we had 'gangs.' Not like today's 'gangs,' just buddies. The older gangs didn't want us younger guys to go with them.

My brother Jerry and I were the youngest, in our pre-teen years, would take our personal frustrations out in a field of 'Butterflies,' on some Sunday afternoons. YES! Believe it or not, we did face frustrations even in our pre-teen years. Hell! We didn't like sleeping in the same bedroom with the ol' man and mom either!

The field was loaded with attractions to butterflies? We would chase them all over that field! We didn't want to hurt them, or kill them, we just wanted to run after them as fast as we could…screaming as loud as we could, every cuss word ever known to mankind, at that time. In fact we invented a few new ones. We did feel much better after that.

I shouldn't mention these following events, because we were bad little boys. But, I want to be as honest and truthful about everything that we did.

Jerry and I would set this same field on fire! It was bordered by streets or alleys. The fire couldn't spread to houses or any structure of any kind. Plus, no trees in it. After we lit the weeds and brush on fire, we would run as fast as we could up an alley behind our house, which was less than a block away. Then we'd wait for the sirens and the bells of the fire trucks coming. All the kids in the hood would run toward the fire, we would also…as if we didn't know who could've done that?

That was always a 'main attraction' event! You have to forgive us, we didn't have E-GADS.

While I'm going to confession here, I might as well tell you about this event.

There was an electric over head power line that ran the street-car, which was on steel tracks in the middle of the street. That electric power line was anchored to the exterior of the rear end of the street-car by a very strong rope. There was a street-car 'stop' at the corner of our street.

When all of the people were cleared from getting on or off, the conductor closed the doors and then take off.

There was a row of hedges that ran along the house on the corner where the 'stop' was. We'd hide behind them. SO! When the conductor closed the doors to take off, we'd jump out of those hedges and pull that electric power line off of the over head electrical connector!

He would have to get off of the street car and come back to the exterior rear of the street car, and re-connect the power line. (*WE'RE NOT THROUGH YET!*)

As soon as he closed his doors the second time, to take off, we'd jump out and pull it off again! Then run home.

Occasionally, we did it during rain and snow storms. *Mea culpa mea culpa! (We're not through yet!)*

The alley behind our house, was about one hundred yards before that 'stop.'

We'd hide in that alley, always in the darkness of the night, and throw snowballs at the street car as it slowed down for that 'stop.'

Once, when the snowballs weren't 'snow' balls, they were 'ice balls!' It was one of those wet snows. Four of us were ready to 'Fire when ready Ridgley!'

36

All four of us hit that glass front window of the streetcar…where people were waiting to get off, and it was shattered to pieces! Needless to say, we all crapped our pants when we actually saw what had happened! We took off running as far away as possible. But, we could see the street-car was still sitting at the 'stop.' There was no EMS back then. Soon the street-car left. Evidently, no one got hurt from the flying glass? *(Mea culpa, mea culpa mea **moxie** culpa!)*

Keep in mind here again, we still never even had a TV at this time! So what else was there for us to do? Yea, right! I honestly believe that those escapades were the worst things that we had ever done! Question here: WE wonder? How does our 'bad-ass' teenage actions match up with today's teenagers? In my opinion, we never even dreamed of committing any serious crimes!

For normal and pleasurable activities, in our backyard included; A three hole golf course, made with #2 Hunts tomato cans. A marble's shooting ring. A basketball hoop on the front of the shed, made from a bushel basket, with the bottom cut out. We also played a game called "Lumbly Peg." Nobody knows why it was called that? It was played with a pocket knife.

All participants would sit on the ground in a circle, with your legs crossed in front of you. With the blade open, you'd use your right or left hand, with your hands crossed over your chest, the knife held in a position under your ear, and flip it to the ground. If it stuck in the ground, the 'player' on your right would have to do it in the exact same manner as you did! It was similar to playing 'horse' in basketball. Are we having fun yet?

Let's pause here a minute.

Put yourself in our shoes. That was all of our outdoor entertainment! Except for playing "Dainty" out in the street, and skinny dipping in the nearby creek, that carried raw sewage.

Those previous events, the street-car episodes, the burning of the field, were the worst episodes of being a mischievous teenager EVER for us. Including all other 'gang' members.

We had three different 'gangs' in and around our street only. Each gang had an average of maybe five guys in it. That's about fifteen teenagers. Not one of us were ever challenged by the cops or our parents for ANY even a misdemeanors! Or any serious acts of being mischievous!

I would venture to say that our 'gangs' were typical of all neighborhood 'gangs' back in our days!

Admittedly, some neighborhood gangs had conflicts…mainly the intrusion of our girl friends. We protective them.

There were 'hints' of bullying around in the school yards. However, not a serious threat of physical, or mental harm to be alarmed about. For instance, our brother Bob the oldest, was a 'victim' of the most serious nature of bullying at our school. Since our family couldn't afford to pay the cost for us to eat at the school cafeteria, we had to run home for lunch. Mom would have a bologna sandwich waiting for us on the kitchen table. The four of us would split two bottles of cola between us. At these times, most all cola's were in twelve ounce glass bottles only. No plastic containers yet? So, we had six ounces of cola for each of us. That was our lunch. We'd eat as fast as we could and then have to run back to school before the bell rang.

WELL! Bob's bully would hold him at the school yard when the bell rang to go home for lunch! That would make Bob late getting back to school before the bell rang. So, Bob was punished by the nun. Bob and the bully both went to the same high school! And the bully kept on messing with him. Finally Bob took a round-house swing at him, but missed him! BUT! That was the last time that he ever bother Bob again.

It was unfortunate for Bob. He was the oldest brother, and the first one of us to graduate from the eighth grade. The next year, (Bob now in high school) we found out that our first cousin, ironically, his name was Ray Wolf! Guess what? He was the biggest bully ever known in our school! Whenever some one 'messed' with us, we'd say: "Hey, buddy, you know who Ray Wolf is? He's our first cousin!" They'd respond; "You boys have a good day." As they walked away.

That's what we were taught! Fight back, don't let him bully you! It works! And yes, there were some fisticuffs, and in the hood, but rare. On occasion, they'd use brass knuckles. Sometimes, instead of brass knuckles, they'd use a roll of nickels in the grip of their hand. Brass knuckles were made out of brass, and had four rings on it for your four fingers. Fights with knives and guns were unheard of.

And NO! You didn't have to steal a gun, rob a bank, rob a person, murder someone…rape a human being…to be a member of our 'gangs.' *Maybe, eat a very small bite of dirt to be a member.*

In addition; We obeyed the law! We knew and understood, without a doubt, that if that law enforcement officer shouted: "STOP OR I'LL SHOOT" We would have frozen in time, with our hands up as far we could reach! (*"Remember the pottery kiln? Yep, that's exactly where we learned all about that part of life!"*).

However, none of us ever got that close to being in trouble. To be perfectly honest here, there was a delicatessen, just past where the street-car stop was. That's where all of our gangs would meet…remember? It was our "Safe Place," similar to 'Arnold's Drive In,' *(Not ALL at one time, just whenever?)* We were like the TV show, "Happy Days."

We really didn't have a "Fonzie" But we could've been the entire cast of that show! *"Our modesty and our virginity!"*

Let me set the scene here. There would be maybe five-to-ten of us teenage boys standing out in the front of 'Arnold's' (the street-car stop) drinking cokes, and eating chips etc…, just watching the world go by, but more importantly, watch the girls go by! Now compare our 'culture' to today's culture.

When a pretty girl got off of the street car, or walked into the store, we'd give her a 'Wolf Whistle.' That was a whistle that you did with your lips and mouth only, there was no physical whistle. She would give us that shy and bashful smile and show approval of our attention.

When she came out and walked away from us, noticing her swing and swagger, we'd say out loud: *"I sure would like to have that "swing' on my front porch!"*

We had other similar compliments about their beauty, or body. And, they loved it! We dated most of them, and they'd tell us that they loved that attention! Who wouldn't? *Sorry guys, and girls, you can't do that in today's world!*

During our teenage years, it was dating times! Many of us dated, and married our childhood sweethearts, I did. The 'culture' back then, was that you lived at home until you got married! No moving into apartments or condos. In addition, you never even thought about having sex until you tied the knot!

Your first challenge or goal, romantically, was to give, and get a kiss from your date. And, that was it! NO touchy feel'ly stuff either, until you did tie the knot. That knot was so tight, it nearly choked us to death! We didn't want to die that early, so we toughed it out! three brothers and I were married over sixty years!

Even though that 'knot' was choking, it was well worth the wait. It's unfortunate that today's generation doesn't honor virginity to be a factor in life, as we did. For both man and woman to be virgins until married…heaven could only be a half of step away from your honeymoon. Moreover, it is the door mat to heavenly bliss for the rest of your life.

Whether you were married or not, we could walk anywhere we wanted, day or night or the wee hours of the morning, in any of the neighborhoods, the movie houses, restaurants, churches etc.. Mass shootings, at entertainment venues, work places, churches, and God forbid schools, were not even dreamed of!

There were NO MASS shootings of any kind! NO ONE would ram their car or truck into a crowd of people.

POP-UP! If you are a millennial, why do YOU believe these shootings occur today? My question here: Could it be from all of the violent 'Games' on your E-Gads! In the movies? On TV? All of us 'GG' guys are praying for you guys. I tell my kids; today's world isn't my world! "What happened to MY world!" Maybe you guys can come up with some reasons why mass shootings do happen, and take proper action to control your E-Gads? There's no answers at this time.

At this point, let me make one thing perfectly clear. My generation is not suggesting that The millennials, baby boomers, and gen x's, to live the way we lived. That can't happen! Never will!

Caveat: But surely we do expect all of the above to examine their consciences. The severe depth of immorality in our country today, is unfathomable.

Morality, dignity, and respect for each other IS the answer. The 'code of honor' must be reinstated.

Side Note: If you haven't learned a little something yet, on what you have just read, that's my bad. It was all about discipline! AND, Obedience!

We never had all of the E-Gads that kept us 'diss' from our family and friends. *(When I use those 'cool' words, like 'diss,' 'my bad,' etc.' it's with 'tongue in cheek.) We didn't use those words.* Hey! No harm no foul.

Our compassion, and love was subtlety and effortless inherent in all of us.

Will today's generation ever be able to restore that condition of love and dignity for one and all others again?

I mentioned earlier, that no generation in the future will ever be as loving, considerate, compassionate, understanding and helpful to each other as ours was. Here's why!

Your E-Gads have been raised over and above of all of the virtues mentioned here. Like it or not, it is another god…another idol. You cannot live without it! It's your heart and soul! Your love, your compassion, your consideration for family and friends are secondary to your E-Gads. WHAT? "Frank" is back! Then, why don't you call, stop by and SEE: mom, dad, brother sister, grandpa, grandma, grandkids, and your friends? While you can?

Based on the past fifty years, your future will be full of the *LATEST* E-Gads, Robots…Human beings as we know them now, will never be the same.

Did you hear that? *IT WAS THE SKY FALLING!* Just kidding, Henny Penney was crushed many years ago by a piece that did fall on him.

Seriously, I believe that we all can agree, it is the *VALUE* of love, affection, compassion, consideration, and care for each other has taken a serious beaten, with the association of the E-Gads.

Sure, all of the above virtues are still alive, and well, and kicking, but very tarnished, lackadaisical, and fading.

Chapter 3

(Traits of the Families)

Have you ever seen the after math of a hurricane, tornado, or earthquake? If you have, you couldn't help but notice the thousands of electrical workers who were dangling from; ladders, hot and dead wires, 'modified' tree trunks, and 'cherry pickers.' You couldn't help but notice that they were all wearing 'Tool Belts' around their waist that included every possible 'tool' needed to restore the power to each and every electrical junction box in every neighborhood.

Let's all assume that we all are wearing that same type of 'tool belt,' but instead of 'tools' for electrical restoration, it is 'tools' for the restoration of sanity, morality, integrity, and consideration for our fellow man in today's world. The leaders of The Greatest Generation wore their belt of 'Tools' proudly, and displayed them in their actions…not in words that wavered with the wind. We'd all like to think that our clergy has his or her 'tool belt' filled to every notch in their belt, with every tool needed to help all of us restore all of the above virtues. Unfortunately, some of us, even the religious sector, are not 'equipped' with the exact same template of tools.

Aside; I heard a meteorologist say: "Every snowflake is the same…but different." Ponder that. Is that a description of each of us also?

Are we so different that we can't stay intact? Can't we weather inclemency, when the going gets tough?

Why is a snowman always depicted with a carrot for his nose, when it's suppose to help his eyes?

For instance: Many of us want so badly to forgive a person for what they had done to us, or what we had done to them. Even though our 'tool belt' is full of virtuous tools, maybe some of are not 'equipped' with the forgiving tool.

Metaphorically, both parties will carry that hatred for a lifetime. Regrettably, if even one party would have been equipped with the 'forgiving' tool, that burden could have been lifted.

How many of us are experiencing that same situation? Fathers, mothers, sons daughters, grand and great grandsons/daughters who do not show up for; Christmas Holidays, family birthdays, weddings, family reunions. All because of some conflict between family members, who are not 'equipped' properly. We really don't have to be apostolic, just common sense-wise.

There is plenty of help for all of us. Just remember whoever said these words: "Sticks and stones will break my bones, but "WORDS" will NEVER harm me." Most often, that's all there is: Just "Words." Sounds very simple doesn't it? But in reality, it is not.

However, if we can keep a positive attitude 'tool' on our belts it will become a standard operational tool. Wear your 'tool' belt proudly, and openly. Not under a bushel basket. Let your little light shine.

Like our mom and dad always told us: "Nip it in the bud." That is; if you can see and/or sense that a conversation is heading toward a sensitive area in our own personal life, yours or mine, you get out the pruning sheers (tool) and snip it immediately. Oh yes, everybody should have a pruning sheer on their belt. They are S.O.T, *STANDING OPERATIONAL TOOL*. It's in your *"FAMILY"* manual.

I had three siblings all brothers, no sisters. All of us were about two years apart in age. Our parents were Catholic; from cradle to the grave. Back in those days, raising a family, you followed a 'Rhythm System.' (So did we four siblings) followed that system to the "T."

Aside here. That rhythm system was just another notch on the GGE tool belt. *Discipline!* Patients! *SUFFERING!*

Recently we lost two of our oldest brothers, during the past six years. Both were over ninety years old.

At no time in our lives did we ever have an argument, a fight, or any conflicts between the four of us.

During our 'productive years,' we gave birth to fourteen off-springs. The oldest brother Bob had two girls only. The second oldest sib, Don, had three girls and a boy. The third oldest, that's me, had three boys and one girl. The youngest one Jerry, had, three girls and one boy.

All of our off-springs are "Baby Boomers." And yes, you guessed it. No arguments, no fights, and no conflicts even now…between all TWENTY TWO of us! We are so proud of that!

Here is a short synopsis of how we lived the way we did.

During our productive years, EVERY SUNDAY, based on the geography of our homes, (called GPS in today's world) we'd pack all the kids into the four cars, filled with picnic gear.

When we all gathered at the last home to go 'somewhere,' we would at that time decide where to go. The kids liked that suspense or surprise. Many times it would be at a local city/county park.

That process was democratic, the majority ruled. On a few occasions, we'd choose a State Park.

(Being transparent here.) We did have a 'whistle blower' in the family.

The oldest off-spring, Bob's daughter, blew the whistle on us!

When she accrued the wisdom of knowing right from wrong, she realized that some of our so-called "State Parks,' that's what we told them…were really the 'rest areas' along the brand new Interstate System! She realized that it wasn't a 'state park,' when all of those big 18-wheelers were parking too close to our picnic tables, and that smell of diesel fluid. *"That is an absolute true story"* Suddenly, all four of our tool belts dropped down around our ankles as if we were chained-gang felons.

However, we did take them to many of our state parks. Mainly so they could swim in a big pool or the many lakes.

In an effort to convince our kids, that we weren't the poorest family in the world. We heard so much about poverty up in Eastern Kentucky, namely Hazard, where the coal miners lived. We toured all of the homes that were tucked inside of the mountains, and their soundings.

Hazard had a lodge named: "La Citadel." They had an Olympic size swimming pool. Even to this day, all of our descendents still talk about that trip. We also enjoyed the great food there, in the restaurant that had a scenic view of the city entire city.

Amazingly, every member of our entire families, from the cradle to marriage, would be together! On every trip!

CHAPTER 4

(Keeping in touch with family)

The youngest brother, Jerry decided to move to Florida in 1959. In 1965, in a caravan of three cars, we headed down to visit his him and his family.

Brother Don and I had brand new 1965 Ford station wagons. Actually, mine was borrowed from my supervisor at work. Bob's was a 1955 four door Dodge.

Here's another 'stamp of approval' for our 'Greatest Generation.' Ask yourself, do you think your supervisor would let you drive his brand new car to Florida? I did promise my boss, that I would replace his tires when he needed new ones. But, he even refused my offer. Evidently, he perceives gifts or favors as I and, most of our generation did If I do a favor for you, or give you a gift, and you return the same favor to me, what have we gained? Let's 'pay forward,' do something good for another person. Back then, people were ready and willing to help each other in any manner they could.

Back to the convoy. Since Bob had the oldest car, I would follow him, in case of an emergency or a breakdown.

Since Don was born with spark plugs where the sun never shines, and a well established auto repairman, he'd bring up the rear.

During most of the driving time, the kids were laying around in the bed of the station wagons playing eight track music, and hanging out over the tail gates. Bob's daughters were switching from one station wagon to the other, after each break at the rest areas.

We did lay-over at a motel on the other side of Atlanta, GA.

What seemed like a trip around the world, we finally arrived at our destination in Florida. We all had reservations at the resort; The Green Heron. Because of a screw-up in our reservations in the hotel section…my wife and I, who preplanned this journey…with a gesture of 'good will' from management, we were given one of the more expensive beach-side villas? At no extra charge!

Legend has it, that on occasions, Ol' Blue Eyes and Ava Gardiner stayed in this exact same sweet!

Of course all of the housekeeping was immaculate. Bed sheets were turned back, with a chocolate on the pillows. SO! Looking for a possible left-over souvenir from the celebrities, (you know what I mean) was not an option.

I did find an empty bottle of Jack Daniels hidden under the bed. It's proudly displayed on my mantel at home. *(LIE)*.

Now, brother Jerry and his family met us at the resort. After all TWENTY ONE of us, (one of brother Jerry's is in the oven at this time) were unpacked and settled in, the kids wanted some ice cream. It was very late at night. We could see down the street, in neon lights, a Baskin-Robins. It was 10:45 pm!

In our battalion-size herd, all twenty one of us trekked along the sidewalk.

As we approached the full clear extra large front windows, encasing the ice cream counter, we were spotted by staff members inside. They attempted to discreetly head toward the front door's locking mechanism! It was 10:55 pm.!

We quickly told the younger kids to get up to that front door as quickly as possible and put on their acting skills of dejection and sadness. It worked!

The manager removed the key, and turned off the alarm, and invited us in. He did lock us in, and turned the sign in the window to 'Closed.' He was tipped well. Question here: How many establishments would do that today?

As happy campers, and licking our ice creams, we all trekked back to the resort for the night. We all agreed that we'd meet at the beach whenever we got up the next morning. No wake up time.

Brother Jerry, now being a seasoned Floridian, was our tour guide and host.

We were treated to a vacation, and tour of the southern section of the entire peninsula, that was second to none.

We ended up with many-many reels of eight millimeter movies of all of our activities. As we speak, they are gathering dust in our keepsake chest. HOWEVER! We had all HARD COPIES of our activities! (not on our I-phones! Just kidding, don't get mad at me.)

Chapter 5

Derby party…Easter egg hunt

(Keeping the family, closely knitted.)

Since brother Jerry and the oldest brother Bob, were handicappers, Jerry and his family would come up for the Derby every year, and stay with them.

Bob's house was only eight furlongs from the finish line at Churchill Downs. Bob and his wife hosted Derby parties for over fifty consecutive years at their house.

In addition, Bob and his wife also held the Easter Egg hunts for over fifty consecutive years.

Naturally, since Churchill Downs isn't open on Easter Sunday, brother Jerry didn't come up for the hunts. He wouldn't drive all of the way up here if he couldn't put a bet up on a horse. Even though Jerry moved to Florida over sixty years ago, he'd call Bob EVERY Saturday morning, just to stay in touch, and maybe handicap a few ponies while on the phone. The two wives finished off the telephonic conversations.

Brother Jerry and I wrote letters to each other once a month for about the first five years that they were down there. Just to stay in touch. At some point in time, he suggested that he would rather call me on the phone rather than write letters. For the last fifty-plus years, and counting, he calls me every

Tuesday night at 7:00 pm., without fail. We've never missed a weekly call. The second oldest brother Don would call him once or twice a month, just to stay in touch also. Course, Don, Bob and I contacted each other every week, or maybe more.

Please! Let us all be honest here. Do you really know of any other family that lived as close as we were, and still are?

The four of us are so proud, and so thankful for all of the blessings that we have received over our entire life. Most importantly, we NEVER had a conflict, or even an argument between us, or any of our first off-springs…from the cradle to the grave. (I can't vouch for our grand, and great-grand kids?)

Although our 'culture' was very unique, many other families lived similarly.

OH! By the way. Brother Jerry has 13 grand kids, and 28 great grand kids! Should I even mention this? One of his first off-springs, left the Catholic church, for the Lutheran church. (We always believed that only Catholics dropped the 'Rhythm System')

For the record: At the present time; Bob has two grandsons, no 'greats,' Don has two grandsons, and three 'greats,' and I have three grandkids, and three 'greats.'
In addition to the above 'family activities' we have also had numerous 'family reunions' both here and afar. Side Note: If you didn't feel love oozing out of your body while you were reading that chapter, then, it wasn't my bad!

Chapter 6

The Civil Rights Movement

Looking back at history, it tells us that Rosa Parks and Martin Luther King Jr. did more for all Americans, white and black, Asian, Spanish, than anyone else, except maybe Lincoln. Just two normal human beings. Yet, not one time in their lives did they ever disrespect our flag, or denounce our patriotism.

How many of us pondered about Martin Luther King Jr. being the president of the United States? Ronald Reagan vice president! How about this picture! Reagan president! MLK vice president!

They have been crowned, by historians! To be the best ever "Communicators" in the history of the United States. God only knows what they could have done for us, and the world, in tandem, during their reign. "Would've, Could've, Should've! Wishes, they'd be here today. We NEED 'communicators.' ASAP! Reminiscing here: Martin Luther King Jr. marched across that bridge with all of his followers. We all remember another man who not only walked with many followers supporting Him, who also knowingly would take the brunt of an attack, at any cost! Even if it would cost them their lives. And it did.

Second to their spirit and determination and martyrdom, they never retaliated, they never disrespected their superiors, nor did they loose their faith and patriotism.

Let me throw the switch to the side track here. And try to explain about how we respected our 'superiors.'

They were; the cab drivers, the street-car conductors, the bus driver, the ushers at the theaters, the manager or owner of a restaurant, the doctor, the nurse, the building manager, and on and on! The school bus driver! More important than all of the above, our law enforcement officers! WE respected all of them, and we did what they told US to do. They are trained to put our safety at the top of their agenda.

Have we ever really stopped and turned our bodies 'off' switch to off? And dug deep into our hearts and minds about why so many human being's are killed or murdered…because we don't obey the command of the law enforcement officer: "STOP! OR I'll SHOOT!" OR! "Drop the gun! When he tells us to! It's such a no-brainer, and so very simple! *YOU CANNOT BE INJURED, OR KILLED! IF YOU OBEY THE LAW! THAT IS; 99.9% TIME!"*

How many 'incidents' happen to law enforcement officers…who are doing their jobs…keeping all of us safe…they do not discriminate when *SAVING* our lives…but loose their own lives for us!

Unequivocally, racism is alive and well in this country today. And that is really sad to say the least. Consolation? I believe that my generation, still has a few racist left in it? Let's be patient. Hopefully racism will die off, like Covid-19. In retrospect, as president Roosevelt asked us to sacrifice, be obedient, and patient during WW ll, I'm suggesting that all of us must be open minded.

I BELIEVE THAT MOST OF US WANT TO PLAY THE MONDAY MORNING QUARTERBACK!

WHEN YOUR HANDS ARE UNDER THAT CENTER'S BUTTOCKS, DO NOT CALL AN AUDIBLE!

LET THE REFEREE SIGNAL… AT THE END OF THAT PLAY…THE OUTCOME OF THAT PLAY. HE IS THE JUDGE. IT IS HIS CALL! BUT1 IT IS YOUR RESPONSIBILITY FOR THE AUDIBLE!

Our sitting president told us, that the escapade in Charlottesville; (White Racist/Nationals) "Both sides had good people in that skirmish."

Does that mean that there were 'good people' on both sides of the Nazi's "Storm Troopers?" The operators of the Holocaust? Being that I was in Germany during my stint in the army, I had the opportunity to visit Dachau, a concentration camp. As I walked through it, I thought to my self, those poor Jewish people didn't have a choice to live. Death was inevitable.

As stated earlier, we must think about our future generations. Can you even fathom what they will think of this generation? When they read history books about this part of their generation's history?

Everyone of us who votes…knows who the rotten politics are! Get them out of there! Stand up and be counted. Whether your state is red or blue!

We all experience moments when we see and hear such a 'change' in policies, or laws, to satisfy our own weaknesses. OH! By the way, you can now 'JUSTIFY' your wrong doings!

It's being done just about every day in this generation's leadership! You commit a crime, but to justify it, you just change it to being 'inappropriate.' Sometimes our emotions overwhelms our ability to describe an experience, when describing it does not capture its significances. That's our problem here!

When we reach a point to *LOWER the bar, rather than RAISING it! We'll never achieve any goal! We become stagnate!*

'Our' mindset was, we can't do a perfect job, that's a known fact. But we must *STRIVE* for perfection.

Unfortunately, this is not the only condition that will be changed to lower our standards, only to satisfy "The Brats."

Definition of; "The Brats!" They are the ones who will never be satisfied no matter how easy their life will be made for them.

It takes place even in our colleges. West Point chose to lower their standards for higher recruiting purposes! They aren't the only ones.

In our public schools? They are lowering the qualifications to graduate? How can we lower our expectations? Shouldn't we all at least 'try' to follow the advice of Kobe Bryant! AND! Many other super stars! Who went over the bar charts!

George W. Bush told the graduating class at West Point: "For all of you who graduated with a 'C-Plus,' there is still hope: you can be the president of the United States!"

Aside here: What happened to my mantra…*If you have to shovel shit…be the best in the world? That is what MY generation was built on! That's MY story, and I'm sticking to it!*

CHAPTER 7

"Social Media, "HELP!""

Let's pause. And try to understand why we don't follow the warnings of law enforcement officers…our parents…our clergy…our teachers…and all of the newscasters! And, don't forget those ever loving meteorologist!

Today's social media warns every one of us to slow down; Stating: "There's ice and snow on the roads that are treacherous! Slow down and slowly brake when necessary!"

They are talking to everyone of us…who have a drivers licenses.

> *BUT! IF WE HAVE EVEN ONE OUNCE OF BRAIN IN OUR HEAD! WE ALL KNOW THAT!*

However? ON national news, there was a pile-up of 131 cars and trucks in Minnesota. True story!

Why didn't those 131 drivers 'obey' that warning? Can you even fathom that happening? 131 drivers! Should we continue warning all drivers, when we never listen? Let us veer off of the highway here and compare why my generation was so different mentality wise, to today's.

Today's social media is constantly filled with warnings of: Extreme weather conditions on our highways and neighborhood streets. The black ice, the deep snow, and sleet! Why do we have to tell this generation to be careful when driving?

They also warn us about 'three layers of clothes, and gloves,' waiting for a bus. Back in our generation the media…the radio…didn't tell us all about that kind of stuff. We knew it, and we dressed accordingly. Why do we have to remind this generation about something that is so deeply inherent! WE knew what to wear when we left our house…because our parents trained us that way. And we added the commonsense, and "Street Sense" factor! *(Again, I wonder? Would it be better not to even warn us about it?)* You don't wear a T-shirt and shorts to sleigh ride in freezing weather conditions! We learned that when we were four-five years old. And yet! This generation has more deaths from freezing, and more homeless people freezing to death, than ever before in history. And more deaths, in the pile-up of cars and trucks on the highways.

> *(I'm reading YOUR mind here. I know what you're thinking: "Don't this dumb ass ninth grader realize this is the 21st century?" Wrong! He does know it's the 21st century, he does know that the cars today are much faster than his. But! He does know…when social media says visibility is practically zero because of the fog…he does not drive at all! And if he does…he doesn't 'tailgate while driving! Someone should have told those THIRTY DRIVERS in California! TRUE STORY! There was a thirty car "PILE-UP" in THE FOG! EVERYBODY WAS WARNED OF IT! A baby was killed in it!*

I warned you; Frank is back!

I am just 'giving you facts ma'am.' Those events didn't happen back in our day. Here's just a snippet of why those conditions didn't take our lives.

Our pot 'belly' coal stove would get as red as a beet! From early morning to near midnight, every day in the winter months. We lived with that stove for twenty years! There was never a guard of any type, to protect us from getting burnt, by touching it, or falling on it…for the twenty years that we lived with it!

Our ages were about two years apart in age. NOT ONE of us ever got burned by that stove! Guess why? Our parents taught us all about danger of touching that red as a beet belly of the stove!

Back in our days', **EVERYTHING started at home!** Only **YOU** know why it don't happen in your home today, so let's change it!

We didn't need anyone in any social media to remind us of danger, or any other condition that could result in a consequent.

> *(WE WEREN'T GADGET DISTRACTED!) We weren't chasing our tails! In today's morning 'rush hour' and evening 'rush hour,' today's driver's, perceive their car, with the motor running, in 'pit-row,' waiting for that pit-crew leader to throw his hand down.*

(Tomorrow morning, when you get in your car, just 'see' that image of Ryan Newmen on the very last lap of the 'Daytona 500 this year' 20/20!).

Every morning and every evening, during rush hour, the city map has pins all over the map where incidents are.

Based on the daily news, of this generations, both local and national, it appears that at least once a week, a child finds a loaded gun in the house, and accidentally shoots a member of his or her own family. Here we go again! Either the chief of police, or the mayor, or the governor is on live TV, reminding us all: Please! "Do not leave a loaded gun anywhere in your house!"

How many days each summer, does a person leave their child in the back car-seat? And dies because of the extreme heat! Maybe the law should change it back to putting the car-seat up in the front seat? BUT! That would be lowering the bar of safety responsibilities. How many more times, will we see life snuffed out of our own children…when it is drilled into our minds and hearts about safety?

What has happened to this generation's concern for safety and saving lives? Even their own! Are we that distracted by the E-gads? OR? Is the 'value' of their lives different than ours were?

On a lighter side. Let's throw a few darts of pun at the meteorologist. Until the 1960's there were only men weather MEN! Our own, home grown; Diane Sawyer finally 'broke the icy ceiling.'

She, and all of her predecessors would report the weather only! NO road conditions about delays, accidents, back-ups, speed to here and there, time to here and there…yet today more people are getting killed on our highways and byways then ever before in our history…even with all of the warnings!
By the way, back in those days, the weather men/ladies used a chalkboard, and a pointer stick to show what the temperature was in each city…not each neighborhood! AND! They didn't point at each temperature in each neighborhood and read it out loud! What difference is it if it's just one degree from another neighborhood? Plus, we can see them!

When the temperature changed, they'd have to use an eraser and change the temp with chalk.

There was no such a thing as a 'jet stream' or a 'wind chill' factor. We found out about tornados, *After they left!*

And yes! With all of the very latest technology, meteorology wise, many still die because we don't follow their warnings!

No offense to the meteorology guys, but in today's world, you guys have way too much air time! Surely, I don't have to tell you why they get that much 'air' time.

In my opinion, the 'newscast' as we knew it, was all about the news. The weather was a fraction of the newscast. That was it. That is, the news, and the weather! No laughing and joking and trying to be funny. Plus, most of the News and Weather was on for thirty minutes only! Not two and three hours long! Other stations had the entertainment stuff.

Have you noticed these type of weather men and women? There's a hurricane heading for Florida! The weather 'person' is wearing waders, and a hoody standing in five feet deep water…the winds are reaching a hundred MPH! They are warning all of us to take cover!!! Stay inside! Why do they do that?

While the weather person is warning us, with rain and wind blowing their cheeks back to their ears, in the background, you can see roof tops blowing across the street, billboards sailing through the air, and traffic lights swinging out of control. All of the while, we are safe inside a concrete structure worrying about *THEIR* safety!

C'mon guys, you're 'stretching' your luck to a breaking point.

Today's alleged 'newscast' is viewed as a 'show.' BUT! More like *a 'variety show.'* Again! I know why, and you do too!

>Example:

>Breaking News! As we come on the air!
>That's the 'routine!' Since everybody is straining for using 'catchy' words, to get our attention, I keep waiting for someone to open with this phase: *Fractured News! News is Cracking!* As we come on the air! The 'Breaking News' as we come on the air!' Will change! They will change that phrase, just as they changed a word that must have been worn out to the threads, that is 'Edit' to *REDACTED! Is that cooler? Or what?*

>Back to the newscasters, it's really a 'variety show.'
>"All three hundred people died in an airplane crash! No survivors! Only the black box will tell what really happened!"

Today's 'newscast' are showing one incident after the other of tear jerking cases of a death because of COVID-19. Without taking a breath, in a split second they switch to a clip from SNL, or from last nights late comedy hours, and everybody's laughing their heads off.

Then it's back to a killing or a stabbing of someone's parents or kids.

Then it's back to laughter and chatter between 'the shows' personalities…and NO one knows what they are saying, because they are 'talking' over each other! *(Sorry guys, I just had to get that out of my system…but it is true!) It's worst today, with all of the reporting of deaths from pandemic of Covid-19!*

However! Back in the day, "Frank" would say: "If the shoe fits, you have to wear it!

Since we're concerned about the problems of today's world, and the lack of a solid cohesive leadership in our present policy makers, maybe a glance back at the leadership of the GG, might be worth another look at.

President Ronald Reagan and Martin Luther King Jr. had two things in common. President Reagan swayed Mikhail Gorbachev to; "Tear down that Berlin wall!"

King, swayed more than 250,000 thousand people to meet him at the Lincoln Memorial, both black and white.

It is ironic, maybe sad, that we would have two icons with similar personalities and convictions. Unfortunately, no one in today's leadership, is qualified to duplicate their credibility!

From president Reagan's famous quotes: "The greatest person is not because he is great, but because he can get other people to do the greatest things."

From Martin Luther King's quotes:

>"The ultimate measure of a man is not where he stands of comfort and convenience, but where he stands of challenge and controversy."

If MLK not be president, or have had a longer life, I would have bet the farm and everything I have or ever had, that the United States would NOT be in such an immoral, disgruntled, feared, hate, and divided condition as it is today!

>*At the ballot box, THIS YEAR! 2020 think about who is the person who is even close to wearing Martin L. King's, or Ronald Reagan's shoes.*

Most likely any political leader, from a mayor of any city, to the richest person in the entire world, could bring the economy to any level he wanted it to be. Also, he could get the trade deficit to any level that he wants it. HOWEVER!

Could he or she! Get us all back to: *Equality *Normality *Respectability *United *Morality *Patriotic? Those roots made us the greatest country ever! Be sure you check those boxes in November! Someone will always be offended somewhere along the way, because we all are like the snow flake. Back in the day, we called it collateral damage.

It is projected that the 2020 census will show there are 350 million Americans living in the United States. 2010 census showed there were 321 million.

Question here. We have over 400 "LEADERS" of this country, and they can't even agree to disagree! How are the millennials going to be able to satisfy 350 million people? Apply it to the present leaders of our country. Where is that core of 'subordinates' in the political world? Where is that base of stability, sanity, teamwork, humankind?

One thing that the millennials must prove is that our entire Constitution, and the Amendments must be upgraded. There must be a law, not an Amendment, the law, that NOT one person can ever shut down the government. Not one person can pardon any felon! Not one person can be immune to the law. Not one person can ever declare a nuclear war. Not one person can ever declare a national emergency.

Let us lay down our arms, our convictions, our hostilities toward one and the other, and open our minds here, in relations to the U.S. Constitution.

The "Framers" were basing "The Constitution" on their culture at that time, and also, maybe the next generation?

Never in their wildest dreams did they ever 'think' of some one going to the moon! Or even a jet airplane! OR, even an airplane with props? How about a drone? How about a robot?

Evidently, their focus was on a president of the United States, who should be above any laws of the land! Why?

There were dictators ever since the world began? More recently Hitler, Mussolini, and Hirohito! Are we being blindsided? As we were by COVID-19? Or, we just plain "Stiffed Necked!"

CHAPTER 8

Discrimination?

Views of both generations

Today's and the Greatest

Thank God for Rosa Parks! Like it or not, she had made this world a much better place than it was.

Did you know that there was a law and/or an ordinance in the City of Montgomery AL during the fifties, that stated a black person will enter the bus in the front door of the bus, pay for her ticket to ride, get back off of the bus, and re-enter through the back door…then proceed to a section cordoned off: "For Colored only"?

That sign: "For Colored Only" would also 'float' over the bus seats? Based on the capacity of the bus. That's were Rosa was sitting. But when the bus driver removed the sign where she was sitting, to seats in front of where she was sitting. Rosa was suppose to get out of her seat, and then stand in the isle, so a white person could sit. She refused, and history was made.

This is a picture of a trolley stop in Louisville KY, 1940's. The picture is not too clear, but those are white people getting on the bus first! Those are black people sitting on that grassy knoll, waiting to board the trolley, after all of the white's were on it. That was the norm. (That is the trolley that we were able to ride to, or from school. Cost was 7.5 cents!) Also, note that steel rod on top of it. That's what we pulled away from the electric power to it! It was tided by a rope on the outside of the rear of it. It was built like that so, the conductor could pull that rod around to the front of it, to put the street car in reveres.

(History lesson here.)

Using that ordinance/law of Montgomery AL, a mere sixty eight years ago, as an indicator of how far behind our leaders are in the acts of The Constitution, and it's Amendments, the leaders of our country as we speak, 2019, has shut down the government in attempt to build a wall similar to one that was built in the medieval times of the fourth century!

Back to Rosa Parks and Martin Luther King Jr., just two normal citizens, within thirteen years, 1955-1968, changed the entire world. That is why they earned their 'charter membership' in "The Greatest Generation !" Lets ponder here. Just two normal, and average everyday citizens…changed the entire world!

King's biography states; his dad used a whip on him until he was fifteen.

Neighbor's states; while whipping him, shouted loudly. "I will beat you until I make something of you, if I have to beat you to death." (That's strong stuff!) BUT! He was being brutally honest and Frank! Well, we all know that answer now. Point here. He was disciplining him! As mentioned previously, that's what makes people great…patients and discipline.

Do you have those two 'tools' on your belt? *MAYBE, just MAYBE, that type of discipline should be re-enacted!*

I'm betting that 'MLK sr.' had them on his belt! Aside, in the fore front, MLK jr. knew life was full of ***"Promise."***

It is the parents that should be held responsible for eradicating discrimination.

In my humble opinion, I would suggest to the leaders of this country to initiate a personalize culture. Meaning, start at home. When that child…black, white, brown, or red, reaches the age of discernment, that parent, single or otherwise, should have a primer book of 'cultures' of all nationalities, the white, black, brown, or red. Have the parents read that book to them every night before bedtime. And, don't stop there. "To be continued:" At a formalized school by the teachers.

When our children enter a learning center, whether it be pre-school, nursery, or the very first grade of formal education, they should be 'fitted' for their "Tool" belt. By the way the tool belt is a one-size-fits all. It needs pruning each year. Nature takes care of the dead sprouts. It automatically drops the tool that has been worn out through the aging process.

These primer books should have some history of the 'culture' of each denomination. EVERY denomination…should be taught in depth…of the laws of the United States of America. That's more important than learning 2 X 2 is four.

In an effort to control or diminish discrimination, we must know each other, and their traits and culture. If we could all take a deep breath here and ponder: We don't fall in love with any human being, any animal, or even materialistic objects…until we 'know' them…or it. We must get to 'know' each other before we can express our love for them.

I'm betting the farm on the following conditions. If each and every white person knew a goodly amount of the history of slavery, put themselves in their shoes…for just a day…discrimination would soon be a thing of the past.

Is this discrimination? As I write, the city of Louisville Ky, has opened up it's third 'Academy' for black people only! This is for Black Girls only. We already have two 'Academies' for Black Boys only! WWWHHOOO NOW! Don't let your underwear get all bunched up in your butt! *AGAIN! This is my opinion only!*

I have been an advocate of this type of educations every since I was in grade school! Grades schools were co-ed. Most high schools were NOT! However, it's those grade school days when we are developing as a human being.

As you know, I was a lanky goofy kid with a high ass! With girls on the left side of the classroom, and us boys on the right side, whenever the teacher asked the entire class a question…us boys, all of us were too embarrassed to stand up and try to answer the question! For fear of being giggled at by the girls if we were wrong. MANY times, we knew the answer, but was afraid to raise our hand. We boys, perceived, that the girls were smarter than we were! Granted! In reality, they were.

Now let's apply this scenario to today's classrooms. There are black, brown, white, girls and boys all in the same classroom. Could any of these kids feel the same way as we did back in our days? Do the blacks feel inferior to whites? Do the boys feel inferior to the girls? Do the Asians and others feel inferior? Visa verse? If so, it could restrict your competence. Caveat! Do not lower the standards for achievement by any means.

Only you can answer that. However! The higher ups in the education system must feel the same as I do? I believe they are really on to something with the academy thing. Check that box! During the greatest generation, pre-civil rights movement, the overwhelming majority of the white population were sympathetic toward the African American community. Because we knew more about their past and their culture.

Here is my personal experiences of living and working with the African Americans.

My great-grand-paw migrated from Germany to Louisville Kentucky. In the 1840-50's, he settled in a neighborhood called "Smoketown." My grand-paw also lived there. Course I had never known my great-grand-paw. They were just a few of the many Germans who decided to follow them to here in "Smoketown.' Soon "Smoketown" was the "German" capital of Louisville, Kentucky.

The reason it was called Smoketown was because it had 18 brick kilns in this area. An area of maybe five or six city blocks, just outside of downtown Louisville. I, personally remember some of the last few kilns that closed up, because that area's land of clay, had been depleted. When those kilns were in full blast, it looked as if it snowed black flakes. The cars and houses were drenched with soot. When The Emancipation Proclamation went into law, migration from Africa doubled and tripled. They also wanted to settle in Smoketown. Soon, it's population was solidified with African Americans.

I can still remember my grand-paw telling us: "I was here before they were, and I'll be here after them, and he was right.

Unfortunately, by the 1960's it was crime infested, many homes were blight.

Back when we were kids, "Smoketown," was thriving.

Grand-paw lived in the middle of the block of East Breckenridge Street. Smack dab in the middle of it. He was the only white family on the street.

He and grand-maw produced eleven children, including my mom. Mom had five brothers, and five sisters. EVERY Saturday night was a beer party. Many of our aunts and uncles could play the drums, and piano…all by ear. Not one lesson between them. They'd roll up the carpets in the two front rooms and would have a ball! Singing and dancing by themselves, or their date?

There was, and still is, a gospel church on the next corner of Breckenridge and Clay streets. You could hear music coming out of every window of that church. No A/C back then. Just handled cardboard fans.

All of us kids, and the Black kids on this street, would be out in the street doing our thing. Dancing and singing. History note here. "Smoketown" is the oldest and most noted neighborhood in the city of Louisville. It is listed in

The National Registered etc. And! The good news! It is a thriving commerce wise and civically as we speak.

Back in 1937, the city of Louisville suffered it's worst flood in history, it is still *THE* record. The Ohio river flooding levels started on January 5, 1937. With grand paw and his family, still living there at that time, the flood water level reached two feet from their interior ceiling! Some of our aunts and uncles were not married yet. Our mom and dad make arrangements for every one of them to be placed in homes that were not flooded…namely ours! Remember now, how small our house was: Two bedrooms, a living room, a kitchen. But, by this time we did had a bathroom on the other side of the kitchen. However! We still had the 'ice BOX'! And only that small pot-belly coal strove for heat!

We had two of our uncles and grand paw and maw maw added to our house. People were sleeping all over the floors etc. etc…Grand paw took over the house and all of it's functions. At bedtime, lights were out! He ruled the roost! The same 'order' was obeyed in the mornings. Mom placed her sisters, and brothers scattered about in the neighborhood. The neighbors were very gracious about helping anybody during these times

These living conditions lasted for well over a month! The Ohio river crested on or near my birthday, February 6, 1937. I was eight years old.

We were grateful that none of our entire family members died or were injured. Unfortunately grand paw's house, and some of his son's homes, near by his house, were extremely damaged.

And again, being very grateful, the city of Louisville, and southern Indiana survived that disaster, just like all others, It made us all closer together than before.

Sometimes we must wonder? Why does it take a disaster of any kind to get us to come closer to each other? Will we *EVER* realize how happy, caring and compassion we can be, pre-catastrophic times?

Since our generation was hit with the evolution of the "E-Gads," We were also hit with the evolution of public discriminatory practices against the Black Community. It tore our hearts out to see the black community living during these times. We knew and they new, they got all of the menial jobs. Many had to shine shoes for a living. Work on garbage wagons and trucks. Be pooper scoopers for the cities and counties.

You might wonder what a pooper scooper's job was…no, not in a barn, or at a race track. The city streets.

Our generation witnessed the tail end of the horse and buggy, and wagon days. The 'buggy' was to transport people, the 'wagon' was for commerce.

At these times the horse didn't wear a diaper as they do in today's world. So, the scooper had to follow behind the horses and scoop it up. Remember what our dad told us about getting a job? "If you must shovel sh— for a living, be the best sh—shoverler in the world."

Referencing the above; I really believe the difference between my generation and today's generation, regarding 'work' ethics, is 180 from each other. We really and truly tried to be "The Best" at what we did, even if it was shoveling shit.

Pull back to the workers during my generation, namely the discriminating years. Many of the women were housekeepers, maids, and servants.

We also saw the black men clean out the bowels of outhouses.

Thanks to Martin Luther King Jr. and Rosa Parks, let's call it the "Black Community" is making headways by leaps and bounds for their community!

However, in my opinion, based on my association with the "Black Community" in my forty years in the work place, as well as family, I worked along side of the blacks, as well as supervising them. Bear with me here now and think a little longer here before draw your conclusion of who I am.

MY RESUME: "STREET SENSE"
(summa cum-laude)

My job was to deliver linens of every shape and form, on a rental basis, to every type of business in the city. My very first route, as a new driver, was at "The Haymarket."

It was an area, mostly for farmers, to bring their products to the market for the retailers. It was a thriving area to say the least.

There were permanent buildings for restaurants, beer joints, whiskey stores, meat markets, groceries, and vegetable stands. And yes, a brothel or two. Some of the farmers wanted to have a good time while they were in town.

In addition to the permanent building entrepreneurs, there were venders who would have push-carts to deliver their products to your neighborhood!

The 'bed' of the push-cart was made out of wood, about ten feet long and four feet wide. It had two handles in the rear of it to push along, and about a foot high board encasing his products.

Most of the venders carried only one item, like watermelons, cantaloupes. Others had multi selections of vegetables.

They would walk down your street, our street was about three miles away from The Haymarket. He'd walk through your neighborhood chanting: "Watermelons! Watermelons! Twenty-five cents each!"

Others would chant: "Green beans, Green beans, five cents a quart, the more you eat, the more you fart!"

It we were playing out in the street in front of our house, mom would say: "Holler out to me when the 'potato man' comes!"

Some of the push cart operators had more of a variety than others.

The overwhelming majority of the owner's of a business in "The Haymarket" were; Greek, Italian, Lebanese, German, Jewish. All fresh immigrants. It was inherent, that as one parent, or family arrived, they would be added to the staff of that families predecessor's business. Louisville was a fast growing city at these times. Soon, each of those businesses would branch out to the growing outer parts of the city.

The Jewish entrepreneurs settled in what was called the lower Highlands, and they also lived in that area.

The Germans, naturally settled in the Germantown area, also known as Schnitzelburg.

The Greeks, Italians, and Lebanese stayed nearer to the original area known as The Haymarket, and Butcher-town. The later was near the Stock Yards for all the slaughter houses.

The majority of the Back entrepreneurs settled in the west end, from fifth street west. They created the 'Norleans East.' They duplicated the French Quarters atmosphere. More on that to come.

Now, here's the road that I'm taking, and I'm sticking to it:
> Remember, I am one month past my fifteenth birthday. I have to learn 'the cultures' of all of the above! I have to know what they expect of me, how they think, what their needs are, and what makes them happy, or mad, and what they think of me...this same ideology must be applied in each of our homes...and our neighbors. This is just one more 'credit' to my resume,' and why my generation IS in fact; "The Greatest!" We were all bounded together.

Humbly, I am happy to report that I serviced this area for three years. I never lost a customer, and I made many new friends along the way.

I also had a route in the heart of the Black Community, known as "Norleans East." It was a version of Bourbon Street in New Orleans. Here in "Norleans" the entrepreneurs were 99% Black. The district was Walnut Street *(Now Muhammad Ali Blvd.)* from Fifth Street west, to Ninth Street.

I served two of the best! The "Top Hat" bar and lounge, and the "Orchid" bar and lounge. Two of many in that district. There were bars and lounges joined at the hip on both sides of the street.

My brother Don had a friend who worked for an amusement company. His friend would service these places with records and music Juke Boxes. He invited us to help him on Friday and Saturday nights to unload the money boxes, add new records, and remove old ones.

Brother Don was a good dancer, and danced with the best of them. He was also a very good drummer with other local bands. We'd have a ball!

The Walnut Street Chili parlor had the best chili you ever had in your life! That was the good times.

However, during these same times, the forties and fifties, there was a large theater on the south side of Fifth Street, facing Walnut Street. It was the National Theater. When it wasn't showing movies, big bands would play there…for all whites only! Naturally, many of the band members were Black musicians. Also remember, it is the 20th Century!

There was a tunnel in the basement of the National Theatre, that ran under Fifth Street, to the Kentucky Hotel…for whites only!

The Black musicians would have to walk, with their instruments, that they could carry…down three blocks to eighth street, south one block to Chestnut Street, to "Hook's Hotel" which was for blacks only.

It's unfathomable that I am still here alive and well, to share this with you. It's also unimaginable that this was happening in the 20th century!

While I was serving 'Norleans East,' I became a very close friend with a black man, let's call him, 'Cleve' Wh! He was a flamboyant entrepreneur! He was ranked up there with one of the best gentleman that I had ever met. He had multi establishments dotted in and around 'Norleans East.' His flagship was the "Epicurean Club." He'd call me on, as needed basis, whenever he needed linens on special occasions. Sometimes the best quality table linens that we had. I was too young to know what clientele he catered to? Other times it was just the regular linens used in lounges bars etc.…

In my twenty years in delivery, 'Cleve' was the only person, black or white, that ever gave me a tip! Nobody ever gave a delivery person a tip in our days! "Cleve' was probably the most well known person in 'Norleans East.'

Unfortunately, "Norleans East" faded away, when the civil rights act went into affect. Fifth Street was the dividing line.

Forth Street was the Mecca of down town Louisville. The Blacks started patronizing the places where they were not invited in the past. They got jobs, shopped at all of the big name stores etc…etc.…

Fortunately, now "Muhammad Ali Blvd." *Formerly; "Norleans East" is a very busy successful business district."*

I was promoted to a position called "Extra Man." Meaning, my job was to fill in on any route where a driver was off sick, or vacation etc.. Two years later I was promoted to route supervisor. I was responsible for seven of the total of the thirty-five routes that we had.

If all seven of my route men were on the job, I would pick out one of the routes and ride with the driver to see how his customer relationship was.

Well, let's call him Tom H. He was a white man, originally from upstate New York. He was in his thirties, and ran a route down in the west end that was prominently black entrepreneurs.

Needles to say Tom was a character to say the least.

He had the best customer relationship of all of the thirty-four other drivers. He was 'unique' to say the least, but you had to like him. He could call you a SOB, or worse and you'd laugh and be his friend.

Surely he was gifted with a 'sense' of who he could use that type of language?

Just about every black establishment he served, he would introduce me to them, with the N-word! Then he'd say something derogatory about them being black! I almost crapped in my pants! But the owners or managers of the business would get a big laugh out of him and the way he was. You had to like the guy, whether or not! Everybody else did. Of course he only did that to be funny. He never had a racist hair on his head.

After a few months as a route supervisor, I was promoted to the "Route Manager." Responsible for all thirty-five routes! I hope you're still with me, here comes the good stuff. I'm not bragging about my promotions, it's my job description. I was asked to take the job as the plant superintendent of the production area. I was responsible for 100 employees…99% were black women! The black men worked in the washroom. There were 10-600lb. capacity washers, that had to be loaded and unloaded manually! Our national office was in Atlanta. They sent a trainer to train me on how the production efficiency is calculated and maintained.

The very first order of business, was that I must learn how to do every job in the production area. And, I had to meet the production standards for each of those jobs! That included the washroom functions also. If you never had to unload a 600 lb capacity washer…full of wet bed sheets… and wet blankets, you have not lived yet. YES! They were still wet!

There was no such a thing as a washer/dryer in commercial laundries. You had to pull the wet linens out of the washer, load them into a steel drum-like perforated canister, that had wheels on it, to a hydrologic plunger water extractor. You ended up with a big solid 'cake' of linens. Take that 'cake' to the dryer, on a roller top canister, and push it off into the dryer.

Then I had to learn how to feed every type of linens through a mangle, with six steaming hot rollers that were 24 inches in diameter. Simply a six roller ironer. Again, if the production standard was feeding 600 kitchen towels through that mangle in one hour, I had to be able to do that. Naturally, I had to know how to meet those standards, because I would have to teach the new employee how to meet the production standards.

After I met those standards, I was told that I must know each and every employee's name, and find out something personal about them, so I can initiate a relationship with them. Under my breath I thought, yea good luck with trying to learn all of their names! However, it took me longer than a month to know their name, but soon it all fell in place.

If you are wondering where I'm going with this, here it is. With 99% black women employees, I had an assistant, a black lady. She would take on the responsibility of training all of the new employees.
Remember the route man 'Tom H.' from New York? This lady was black, from right here in Louisville KY. And she had the same credentials as Tom H. did. The most personal and charming personality you could ever have. She could get along with anybody, black or white, boss or worker. Her name was Anna H. She was in her twenties, I was in my thirties…the 1960's.

Once I asked her why she didn't get something done from her crew. Her response was: "Mr. Ray, some of these F'n N's think they are white people! They think they don't have to work. Believe me, I'll take care of it for you." We both peed our pants laughing over that.

That was the first time that I had to consult with her about a problem. And also, the last time. She always did take care of every problem that I ever had.

I bring this out so this generation can understand how our 'culture' was, in comparison to today's culture. We had a relationship. We had conversations with each other. We soon learned who each of us were. Not only in the work place but in society as well. It appeared to me, and my generation, that the black people were content with their way of life back then.

In the work place, they never bitched about anything, that they thought could've been discriminatory, or degrading. We have to know each other. Period! Anna decided to move to California! I sure missed her. But here's where I'm going with this. She would call me ever so often from California, just to see how I was doing, and we'd talk about our families etc....I don't know if you know where I'm going with those two relationships or not? But here we go.

Both Tom and Anna used the N word as if it was part of a normal conversation… just between the three of us only, not in front of another employee, in public, or in ear shot of anybody else, white or black.

CHAPTER 10

Hardships Of the Greatest Generation's children. Their personal lives.

Our dad, like many American men, was an alcoholic, and our mother was a saint.

He had a steady job all through the depression. Unfortunately, they cut his job back to two or three days a week. However, even with two or three working days a week available, he would lay off to drink…maybe one or two, or the entire three days.

During these years, he had what they called a 'rider.' (Today, they would call that car pooling.) The rider would take four or five to work. All working in the same department…the foundry! It was hell on earth dealing with that heat.

His rider would get to the house about six o'clock in the morning. He'd tell our mom goodbye. But when he got out to the car, he'd tell the rider, 'cover for me.' Meaning I'm going down to the corner beer joint. A neighborhood saloon, where he'd run a tab.

He would stay at the bar all day. He'd come staggering up the alleyway about the same time that he would normally get off from work, about four o'clock. Attempting to imply that he had just got off from work.

The rider and the other riders, were thicker than thieves. And, their supervisor was the boss of the 'gang.' Their supervisor would cover for him, and the others. There was no way in this world our dad could have kept his job with his blatant absenteeism record.

Before anyone wants to throw stones at their dad, let's put your shoe print in his. You have two sons pre-depression years, 'the roaring twenty years,' and two during the depression years. Ages ran from new-born, to eight years old! Plus you have a job in hell on earth. During these same years, suicides busted the charts to kingdom come! Bankruptcies followed in the same manner.

Our dad's actions of alcoholism caused the four of us boys, and my mom, unfathomable times of pain and suffering…mentally. He was never abusive in any manner to us or mom. His drinking was done on the five working days.

When ever he would go to work with his buddies, when they reached the parking lot at the plant, he'd tell his buddies to 'cover' for him. Meaning tell the boss that he is sick. Instead of walking into the plant, he'd walk across the street from the plant, to a saloon there. He'd be tanked out by noon. He could walk home from work, but unstable all of the way home. He'd walk all of the alleyways. He didn't want neighbors seeing him in this condition. Unfortunately, one of his alleyways, was behind our grade school yard.

Our buddies would see him staggering up the alleyway. They'd holler out to us: "Hey Kleier boys, there's your old man…drunk again!" Needless to say, that was very embarrassing to us.

After '*Dinnertime,*' that's on Sunday, with the entire family, he'd ask us what we wanted to do with him? We had three choices. Now listen closely here, you talk about having fun!

"He ask us: Do you want to 'cem, eastern, or creek'? Definition for those three choices: 'Cem' meant take us to the cemetery! Just walk through it, visiting our family graves. He'd tell us stories about each one of them! 'Eastern,' meant just walk along Eastern Parkway, and just talk! Are we having fun yet? 'Creek,' meant walk back along the creek…and just talk. However, here's where we really had fun, we were able to skip rocks across the creek!

Our choice was just one of those 'ventures.' each venture lasted about an hour or more. There were times when one of us would get tired, and he'd wrap us around his neck and carry us the rest of the way home.

Our dad had the build of a real Santa Claus. He used it for all of the kids in the hood.

Because of our restraints financially, when we really knew who Santa was, we were told that we'd have five dollars worth of toys from him. I always liked trains, so I only got one toy, they cost $4.99. People don't believe this when I tell them this condition.

Money was not available for any kind of 'treats' for us. Every penny that dad brought home went for food, or the rent. *(Of course, he got all the alcohol he wanted from the loans at Credit Union at work.)*

Our treats, were every two weeks ONLY!! That's when he brought his check home. The four of us kids got one only, Milky Way candy bar...cut in four bites, one bite for each of us! If we decided to get a popsicle instead of the candy bar, each would get one stick of it only.

On occasions, he'd take us to a big amusement park in the western part of the city. We had to ride a street-car to get there. The token cost 2 for 15 cents.

The street-car stopped at the entrance to the park. We'd get off and think we were going in the park, but all we were able to do is look through the wrought iron fence. He never had money for us to go inside. However! He, and all vets from WW 1 got a bonus from the government. Then he took us inside a few times.

In Summary; It appears that there are a few glaring indicators that can differentiate, why our generation was the greatest ever! And why it will never happen again.

Would you agree that the number one reason is: *Discipline!* Today's generation's tool belt is not equipped with that tool. In my opinion, there are two definition's of discipline. One physical, and the other mentally. It appears that most of the country has discontinued the use of the physical aspect of it. That is 'paddling,' and 'hand whipping.' Both of which I disagree with.

But, it made my generation the 'greatest,' and produced myriads of the 'greatest' human beings ever known to mankind!

I'm here to testify that physical discipline does work. ***"THAT IS, IN MODERATION!"*** Dad used his hand, ***NEVER*** his fist, on our butt, legs, back, arms, hands… ***NEVER*** face or head.

Remember in earlier references to my younger brother and me, being bad-ass kids? The abuse of the streetcar conductor! The (ice) snowball episode! Setting the field on fire! Etc.…Well, we also stole the best tasting cherries that you have ever tasted in your life. The punishment that we received from dad, over those cherries, made us who we are today. Brother Jerry is 89 years old, I'm 91 years old. Humblebragging" here again. Brother Jerry has 13 grandchildren, and 27 great-grandchildren. I have six grandchildren. Neither of us had even the slightest brush with the law in any manner, shape or form. We both were truck drivers for over twenty-five years…never had a serious accident…in a truck or our personal car…not even a parking ticket. Case closed.

"Humblebragging." Bear with me here, and step back into my shoes just one more time. You'll appreciate this.

During the year 1968, in our new plant fully staffed, there were riots in the entire city. Homes and cars were sat on fire! The Civil Rights movement. I only bring this up for this reason only: We had 100 employees, all black and of numerous denominations of religion. Our General manager of the plant was Jewish, I was Catholic. My boss knew a Baptist preacher who worked across the road at International Harvest. He asked the preacher to come over to our plant and pray with us. My 'office' was on a stand-like, elevated about two feet off of the floor. Similar to a small stage set. EVERY morning that preacher would come over and lead us all in prayer. Every employee attended…it was not mandatory.

I'm so proud of the fact that there was NEVER one incident of any kind at the plant during those trying years.

Evidently, it was at this time, that I was 'coming out of my shell'? ***"THINGS"*** do happen!

Our boss, was transferred to a plant in Knoxville TN.

Reflections: Good luck Millennials, it's up to you to re-stabilize the world. Best wishes for your future! I would like to leave you with a birds eye view, that could be very helpful to you to scan over.

In my mind's eye, it's the icing on the cake of my life. Maybe you can follow my road to happiness.

I hate to use <u>I</u> about this, but <u>I</u> am so proud of my achievements…mainly because of my background in education, my low esteem, and living in poverty, in my early years!

If you have struggled with these same conditions, or similar, and can follow in my footprints, you will feel more proud than ever.

RECAP
"Each Step Along The Way."

The fall of 1943: Employed as a helper on a laundry/linen truck.

June of 1944: Promoted to a driver.

July of 1946: Promoted to: "Extra Man." My duties; fill in on all of the routes, when the regular drivers were off for vacations, sick days, etc…

January 1947: Promoted to Route Supervisor: Responsible for seven routes.

January 3, 1951: Reported to Uncle Sam for two years during the Korean War. Came back to my job as route supervisor.

January 1960: Promoted to the Route Manager…of all routes!

May 1965: Promoted to the plant supervisor of all of the production facility. Responsible for a production crew of 100 employees.

January 1969: Left this job to go into business for my self, and a partner. A laundry and dry cleaning plant. This act was a very deep pothole in the road.

My business partner was my assistant when I was the plant production manager. We knew how to get the job done through people, but we really didn't know the infrastructure of operating a business. Plus we were scammed by the man that we bought the business from.

He told us that all of the equipment in his plant was his. Within a few months time, equipment rental people came by and wanted their equipment! All of his equipment was leased! If there is any consoling, we were his forth victim!

March 1971: Through networking, in the commercial laundry/linen services, my name was mentioned when a brand new Medical Center Co-op Laundry was under construction, near completion.

It was built to service all of the hospitals in down town Louisville, namely the five biggest hospitals of the Medical Center. "They" contacted me! I was hired in as the plant production supervisor.

I was responsible for hiring approximately 85 employees, just to open the plant.

July 15, 1977, I was approached by the executive director of the Down Town Medical Center, to submit my resume for the General Manager of the entire plant. *(EXCUSE ME WHILE I GLOAT A SMITEN HERE)*.

The resume called for a college degree, with a MBA!

I told the Exec, about my education, but he already knew that I never graduated from High School. He told me to submit my resume anyway. He was the one who hires General Managers. But it would also have to be cleared by the executive committee of the five hospitals. We had two other GM's before me. I as hired as the general manager!

Neutrally, it was my past experience in this field that I got the job.

No offense here to all of you guys that were lucky enough to get a college education…But! If I DID have a college education with a MBA, I surely wouldn't be running a laundry!

With my executive director, every month we would meet with the president or the CEO of each of the hospitals. I would make a presentation to them about the operation of the laundry. Such as; why the cost was whatever it was, and suggest making changes to enhance the operations.

One of the biggest suggestions was installing an electronic counter…to count all of the soiled linen that came into the laundry…which I invented. It was placed into operations and both parties, them and me, would share in any profits that would be made, when selling it to the other laundries.

At this time, our annual budget was north and south of 3 Million dollars. They had never disputed my projected budget!

I sort of had them by the short hair here…NONE of them ever had experience in operating a commercial linen/laundry service.

Reflection here: Just put yourself in my shoes. Here I am; a dumb ass, uneducated, with the lowest esteem known to mankind…who was thrust into a poverty stricken environment. Now, here I am soothing and comforting a dozen or more top executives in a conference room.

It wasn't long, after I was hired as the GM, I found out that the association we belonged to…Every one of those GM's had those credentials? That is, a college degree with a MBA.

The association was called: American Cooperative Hospital Laundries. We were all non-profit organizations, (501c3) We had 55 members scattered across the country, and three in Canada.

> *(EXCUSE ME FOR GLOATING JUST ONE MORE TIME!*
> *BUT PAY ATTENTION HERE, THIS IS FOR ALL OF YOU*
> *WHO HAVE THAT SAME FEELING THAT I HAD WHEN*
> *I WAS GROWING UP.)*

Every six months we had a meeting of the association, rotating from one plant to the other. Since we were non-profit, we weren't competitors, we shared our operational activities with all of the members.

It included the most efficient operations: Ranked on how economically your operation was. My plant was always in the top ten, one year I was ranked second. But! That's not what I'm most proud about, here it is, if you haven't already figured it.

My plant was the host of the National meeting of the association in August 1985.

Naturally, the host plant GM, would have to get up at the podium and address the entire 55 members, all of them had a college ed, and a MBA! Guess who that was? YES! ME!!!

So, if you think you can't do what ever you really want to do, just remember me, a dumb ass, with a high ass, with wild hair, with the lowest esteem known to mankind, self consciousness, and full of anxiety.

In December 1985, I got the best evaluation ever…on my job performance … from the executive director, my boss!

On January 1, 1986, I got a raise of 11% in my salary! THAT amount of raise in pay was unheard of at that time.

August 12, 1986 (seven months later) that same boss fired me! He used a clause in my job description: "Either party can terminate with 90 days severance pay." (I must've really pissed him off about something?) I filed a lawsuit against the medical center, and THEY settled! You know what 'they' always say; if I can do it, you can also! GO FOR IT!

Attention Millennial's.

You are on the brink of changing the entire world! Today!

This year, 2020 has sat the stage for you, and you alone. You are the "Hamilton" of our society! And, this generation!

With COVID-19 sitting in the balconies, the entire audience is banned together with love, affection, hope, and inspiration, awaiting your performance.

You must capture the essence of the audience while that aroma is still fresh and gloriously engrained in their hearts! They must carry that feeling with them!

When the curtain closes, let your garments lay in the dressing room.

Look for a bigger stage. Be REAL leaders of our world! We are counting on you! You can do it! You have the tools! PLEASE use them!

Be our heroes!

Mr. Kleier is a member of the "Greatest Generation!" His writings are a testament of why it was deemed "The Greatest."

Prior to the infiltration of the catastrophic COVID-19, this generation was already in the pits of division.

Mr. Kleier's comparison of his generation to this generation…the later could go down in history as "The Worst" generation…based on the C-19 out come?

On the brighter side…this generation can be, and hopefully will be…"The Greatest Generation EVER!" If they can bring this country back to normalcy, sanity, and morally grounded.

Fortunately, it will come from the lowest level of the pyramid of hierarchy. The people of the United States of America.

"We can do it!"

That was the motto since 12-7-'41. We all came together! And we did do it!